MW01632656
EXCLUSIVE
JURASSIC
WORLD
DOMINION
INTERVIEWS
COLLECTOR'S EDITION
Entertainment
WEEKLY
THE ULTIMATE GUIDE TO
Jurassic Park

Dr. Alan Grant (Sam Neill), Tim (Joseph Mazzello) and Lex (Ariana Richards) in 1993's *Jurassic Park*.

Contents

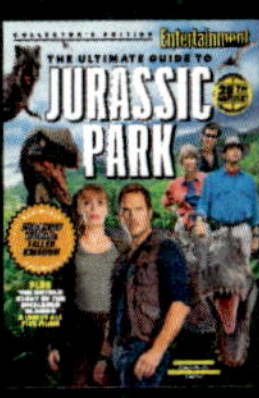

Parts of this collector's edition appeared in this 2018 issue of *Entertainment Weekly*.

WHY DINOSAURS RULE

Many had feathers instead of scales—but does it really matter in the end? Here's why Steven Spielberg's vision for dinosaurs is the only one that counts. **BY ALYSSA SMITH**

BY THE TIME THE TYRANNOSAURUS REX makes his terrifying entrance onscreen in 1993's *Jurassic Park*, audiences were sold on Steven Spielberg's larger-than-life vision of prehistoric, meat-eating beasts.

But today we know that many elements of those onscreen dinosaurs were based on outdated and inaccurate information. New scientific discoveries made since 1993 have revealed that dinosaurs likely had more feathers than scales, the Brontosaurus never existed (and then, wait, they existed again), and thus far no one has ever been able to obtain petrified DNA out of amber.

The beasts in *Jurassic Park* were not intended to be fictional. Spielberg notably brought in paleontologist Jack Horner, who served as an adviser on the series, to keep his dinosaurs more or less accurate. But there were always parts that were a bit more fiction than fact.

Colin Trevorrow's first Jurassic film, 2015's *Jurassic World*, retcons those inaccuracies and gives BD Wong's Dr. Henry Wu a chance to remind viewers that the dinosaurs were never exact—on purpose. "We have always filled gaps in the genome with the DNA of other animals," he says, referring back to the frog DNA they used in *Jurassic Park*.

Dinosaurs have been a source of fascination ever since the first giant fossil was unearthed in 1819. Part of what makes Laura Dern's Dr. Ellie Sattler and Sam Neill's Dr. Alan Grant (who is based partially on Horner) so compelling is they had spent their lives digging in the dirt, piecing together old bones and wondering "what if?" And then, suddenly, they (and the audience) didn't have to wonder anymore.

Dr. Grant can't stop marveling at the living beasts even after his hair-raising encounter with the T. rex. The swarm of Gallimimus he and the kids encounter move "just like a flock of birds," he says in reverence. And even after the T. rex chomps down on one: "Bet you'll never look at birds the same way again."

Of course, after a few more close encounters, Dr. Grant reevaluated his misplaced affection for the resurrected creatures. But audience's fascination with the giant beasts had just begun.

Would velociraptors be as scary if they had feathers, like we now know they did, and perhaps looked more like an enormous goose? (Quite possibly—ask anyone who has been attacked by a particularly pernicious waterfowl.) A few feathered dinosaurs will appear in Trevorrow's 2022 film *Jurassic World Dominion*.

But in the end, does it truly matter? After all, *Jurassic Park* spawned not just a new generation of filmmakers who wanted to make movies, but a new generation of paleontologists who wanted to learn about *real* dinosaurs.

We know so much more about these prehistoric beasts today than in 1993 partly because of *Jurassic Park*. The future scientists that left those theaters have gone on to make discovery after discovery and have ushered in a golden age of prehistoric science. On average, more than 40 new species of dinosaur have been unearthed each year since 2003, more than six times the number discovered in 1990.

And along with those new creatures—some large, some small—have been dozens of other facts. Velociraptors were much smaller than depicted onscreen and far dumber (thank God). The Dilophosaurus probably never spat venom. But honestly, it doesn't matter. Audiences love this version of dinosaurs. Spielberg managed to do more than popularize dinosaurs; he inspired a generation of scientists. And many more of them, like Dr. Sattler, are women.

Let's just all be grateful that if a real T. rex is ever cloned, you'll be able to outrun the feathery beast. Paleontologists today agree that a T. rex would not move faster than 3 mph, or about the pace of a brisk walk.

Steven Spielberg and Kathleen Kennedy, on-set at Jurassic Park, next to the practical effects Triceratops.

Left: the Archeopteryx fossil, first discovered in Germany in 1861, that linked dinosaurs to birds. Right: a modern depiction of a raptor.

DOMINION

All Together Now

DIRECTOR COLIN TREVORROW UNITES LEGACY AND RETURNING CAST IN A RIVETING CONCLUSION TO THE ENTIRE JURASSIC FRANCHISE. AND YES, THERE'S A T. REX. *By Bill Keith*

EXCLUSIVE: **INSIDE THE NEW FILM**

From left to right: Kayla Watts (DeWanda Wise), Maisie Lockwood (Isabella Sermon), Claire Dearing (Bryce Dallas Howard), Dr. Alan Grant (Sam Neill), Dr. Ellie Sattler (Laura Dern) and Owen Grady (Chris Pratt).

WHEN JEFF GOLDBLUM'S BELOVED WISEASS Ian Malcolm asks, "Why do they always have to go bigger?" in the *Jurassic World Dominion* trailer, he could be talking about the dinosaurs. Or he could be referring to anyone tasked with making the latest enormous installment of the Jurassic Park franchise.

But this time around, things were unexpectedly quieter at first, if ultimately no less rewarding. After five movies and nearly 30 years of Jurassic filmmaking, and despite being shot in the midst of the COVID-19 pandemic with limited crews and tightened timelines, the sixth film surprised even the most seasoned actors. "The fun that we had on *Dominion*—despite everything that was going on in the world—it's like the first movie times a thousand. And the first movie was a once-in-a-lifetime thing!" says Bryce Dallas Howard, who has played Jurassic World executive-turned-dinosaur-activist Claire Dearing for nearly a decade now.

It's just what writer-director Colin Trevorrow—who wrote all three *Jurassic World* films and directed the first—was going for. "The first film was more structured, partially because I had this massive production on my shoulders," he says. "On this one, I got to go back a little bit to the way that I did *Safety Not Guaranteed*," he says of the 2012 Sundance Film Festival and Film Independent Spirit darling he directed before being given the Jurassic reins. "As I make more movies, I understand that there are certain ways that I work that make me more comfortable. It may have felt like movie summer camp, but that's just where I feel at home."

Some of that summer camp environment was by Trevorrow's design, but COVID-19 delays and the resulting isolation that forced cast and crew to idle in a hotel together for weeks at a time created a beneficially intimate environment for all. "We shot the film chronologically," says Chris Pratt, who portrays the franchise's resident raptor trainer Owen Grady. "In many cases I wasn't in scenes with some people until the third act, but by the time we were all on-set together, we'd already had boozy wine nights and long dinners and walks and talks around the grounds of our hotel."

Mamoudou Athie (*The Get Down*), who was one of a few key newcomers to the franchise and who makes his Jurassic debut as biotech exec Ramsay Cole, says the closeness also fostered an improvisational process that unpredictably changed the direction of his character entirely. "Colin was really awesome about taking in all of our feedback. My character couldn't be more different from when I got there to what the final product is. I would never think that such an intensely popular and expensive project would be so collaborative."

◀ Dr. Grant, Maisie and Owen face off against a threat.

▼ The beast comes a bit too close to comfort for Kayla and Dr. Sattler.

It helps that it's Trevorrow's style to tell his actors everything about where he wants his story to go. "In my first conversation with Bryce Dallas Howard, I just told her the whole story," he says. "When I want someone to come and give that much of themselves to it, I feel like out of respect I just lay it all out on the table. Obviously I'm opening myself up to scrutiny at that point, but I'd rather be like, here's everything I'm thinking. Let's talk about it. Let's figure out if there are things that you don't feel like Ellie or Alan Grant would do or say."

And speaking of Ellie and Alan, it's no secret that the biggest thrill in *Dominion*—apologies to the Giganotosaurus, Quetzalcoatlus and pyroraptors—is the return of legacy actors Laura Dern, Jeff Goldblum and Sam Neill, who are onscreen together for the first time since 1993. Trevorrow says incorporating them with existing stars Howard and Pratt as well as brand-new players Athie and DeWanda Wise (*She's Gotta Have It*) couldn't have gone more smoothly. "I tend not to audition much," he says. "I find actors who I think are brilliant, then call them and ask them to come be in a movie. That definitely was the case with Laura, Sam and Jeff. It was also the case with Mamoudou and DeWanda and everybody else. Everyone was the first choice."

"It was a thrill ride of collaboration being bubbled up with everyone in that hotel and working on weekends and tweaking the stuff we had to do the week to come," agrees Goldblum. "It was a very fun, collaborative, delicious little endeavor."

Still, the stars of the show are as always the dinosaurs themselves—of which there are many more than ever before in the history of the franchise. "There's a great humility that I have when I think about dinosaurs," Trevorrow says. "There's a line in the first film that Irrfan Khan delivers: 'They remind us how very small we are and how new.' I think when you leave this film, to be able to look at the story we've told and think about what dinosaurs mean to us—hopefully on a deeper level—I feel like they are a reminder that we've been on the earth for a very small sliver of its history. We act like this place belongs to us, but it doesn't. It's belonged to many living things, for arguably billions of years. I think that is an idea that, right now, is important to remember."

"I TEND NOT TO AUDITION MUCH. I FIND ACTORS WHO I THINK ARE BRILLIANT. THEN CALL THEM AND ASK THEM TO COME BE IN A MOVIE"

–Director Colin Trevorrow

▲ No longer simply in isolation on Isla Nublar, dinosaurs are rampaging across the planet and have found themselves in places such as this underground ring (left) and in wetlands (right, stalking Claire Dearing).

◀ Grady calms a captured Parasaurolophus.

A WHOLE NEW PLANET

Director Colin Trevorrow made an effort to use animatronic puppets and real sets for many of the set pieces in *Jurassic World Dominion*. "We don't really rely on visual effects outside the dinosaurs themselves. Everything else is practical," he said. "We built these massive sets." **BY BILL KEITH**

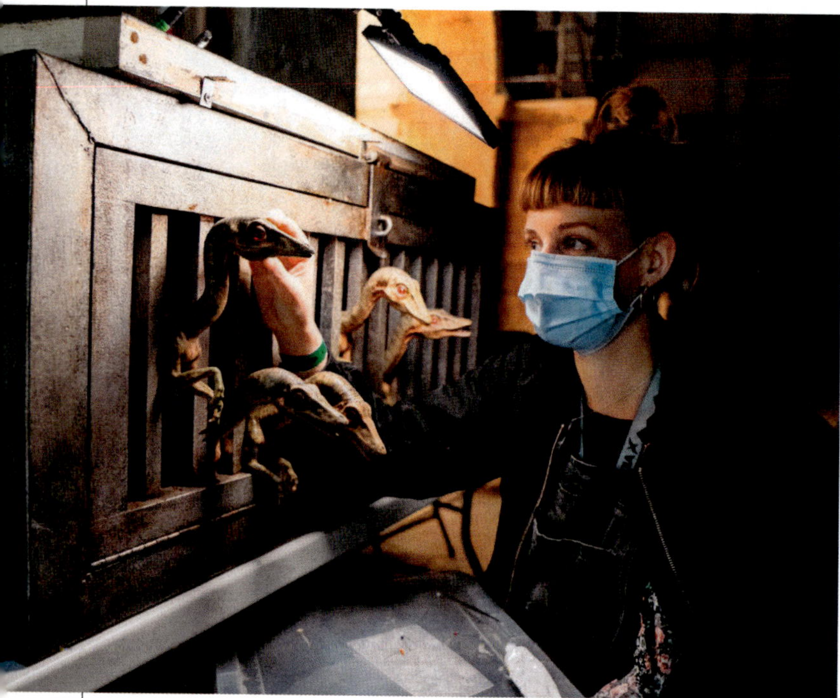

▲ One set—an underground black market selling live dinosaurs—was Trevorrow's favorite. "I think we had 15-plus animatronics going at the same time, with various puppeteers around," he says. "Then all of these extras and this massive set that we built on the bond stage. It was such a complete vision of a fantastical place. It felt so real."

▶ Chris Pratt with one of the new feathered dinosaurs that will appear in the film.

▲ Pratt and Omar Sy take direction from Trevorrow (bottom, in mask). "I think giving everybody, again, a sense of shared ownership is really a theme for me," says Trevorrow. "I hope that everybody walks away feeling that they can really spot their contribution and that it wouldn't have worked exactly the way it works without them."

▶ Jeff Goldblum on-set with Trevorrow, who he described as "so smart, so kind.... He was very generous and was very collaborative."

MEET THE CAST

Character Studies

CHRIS PRATT AND BRYCE DALLAS HOWARD LEAD A STELLAR ENSEMBLE OF NEW AND RETURNING ACTORS THROUGH *JURASSIC WORLD DOMINION'S* OUTSIZE DINO ADVENTURE

PHOTOGRAPH BY MATTHIAS CLAMER

Chris Pratt and Bryce Dallas Howard (and the Indoraptor) photographed exclusively for *EW* by Matthias Clamer on March 7, 2018, at Universal Studios Hollywood.

Chris Pratt

"THIS IS GOING TO OPEN UP WORLDS"

Raptor trainer **OWEN GRADY** acts first and analyzes later. Had the suits followed his advice and evacuated, thousands would be alive. But then there wouldn't have been a sequel. **BY BILL KEITH**

WHEN CHRIS PRATT FIRST STEPPED ONTO the *Jurassic World* set in 2014, he wasn't just intimidated by the enormous sets and gigantic practical monsters he had to contend with. He also had the towering legacy of the franchise's original films lurking around every corner. But after costarring in *Jurassic World Dominion* alongside the legendary actors who starred in the first *Jurassic* films, he finally feels confident that he's lived up to the standards they set some thirty years ago.

It's been seven years since your first *Jurassic* movie came out. Do you remember what surprised you most when you saw *Jurassic World* for the first time?

While we were shooting, I understood that I was witnessing the invention of a whole new medium in digital CG cinematography, but once you saw the CG for real, you thought, "Oh my God, this is going to open up worlds"—it's like the Internet or something. It's just like our imagination is the only limit to what we can do with this now—anything you want to create, you can create.

I felt that even as a kid watching the original movies, not even knowing that one day I would grow up to be an actor. Even then I was thinking, "Wow, they're going to be able to do everything."

What did you need to do differently in the latest *Jurassic* movie?

Skills-wise, you see me doing more horseback riding and more motorcycle racing, but the skill Owen's trying to master now is parenthood. That's really been the natural progression for Owen and Claire through the course of these films. He is becoming less selfish, he's a man who now has obligations beyond the moment, and he's struggling with what all of us who have children struggle with.

You're not a stranger to huge franchises. What makes this one different?

I entered this franchise as a fan at 13 years old and I'm exiting it as one of the lead actors at 43. In those 30 years, this extraordinary and beloved franchise has grown, and I've become a human being who's lived an entire set of lives. That's what makes this unique. I guess maybe people who have been part of *Star Wars* may feel the same way. This was certainly my *Star Wars* growing up.

Did starting your journey as a fan make you nervous to work alongside the legacy cast in the latest film?

When we made *Jurassic World* there was a little, small part of me that was like, "should I not be doing this?" This is a very sacred franchise and we're continuing that on. To meet them and know that they were willing to be a part of this again and to know that they really loved what you did, that in and of itself felt like such an endorsement of what we'd done, which is all we were desperate for.

It was like dating their daughter or something, we needed that blessing. We needed Sam and Laura and Jeff and BD to say: "Great job, guys." If they said that they didn't like it, I would have probably jumped into the Thames River and drowned myself.

I don't think there is anyone out there whose opinion of *Jurassic World* I care more than the legacy cast, so the fact that they signed up to do this one really confirmed my choice to do it in the first place.

> "I ENTERED THIS FRANCHISE AS A FAN AT 13 YEARS OLD.... THIS WAS CERTAINLY MY *STAR WARS* GROWING UP"
> —*Chris Pratt*

Bryce Dallas Howard

"IT IS HER RESPONSIBILITY"

In *Jurassic World Dominion*, former park administrator **CLAIRE DEARING** continues her 180-degree shift from asset loving to dino loving. And she'll keep the stilettos. **BY BILL KEITH**

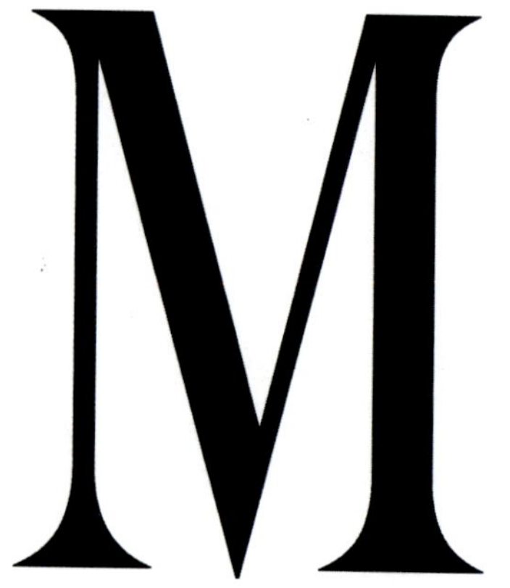

MORE THAN ANY OTHER CHARACTER IN THE second series, Jurassic World operations manager-turned-Dinosaur Protection group leader Claire Dearing has, ahem, evolved a great deal over three films, a process the accomplished actor has enjoyed playing for seven years.

What about playing Claire originally struck you as a unique opportunity?

I've never done series television or played a character that gets to have this kind of a journey and a run over the course of many years. I've done movies where I would come in for the third film or the fourth film, like *Twilight* and *Terminator* and *Spider-Man*.

Claire has had quite an evolution in seven years.

We've seen her go from being a C-level executive and villain in the original, to then become an activist in *Fallen Kingdom*, and then at the end of *Fallen Kingdom*, there's proliferation, so the dinosaurs are absolutely everywhere. It started with John Hammond, but Claire was a huge part of rebooting that park, and it is her responsibility. In this movie it's about how someone can take responsibility for their mistakes but also know that it's not about them. It can't be about them redeeming themselves or the guilt that they feel, because that is not going to always lead to effective change.

You've confessed to being a total tech nerd. What advances have you witnessed over time?

For me, the ultimate magic trick is when there's the convergence of technology that is just starting to be understood and storytelling. When you're viscerally experiencing something and you don't understand it but you just know it's true, when your body feels something that logically your brain doesn't understand: That to me is the most exciting part of our work.

But...and now I love this too...when we shot the dying Apatosaurus in *Jurassic World*, that was an animatronic. The sentiment at the time was that a CG dinosaur would be better, and there was even talk on the day of needing to replace it [in post]. And I remember being like, "What are you talking about? Like, look at this! To the naked eye, it's real."

None of the Apatosauruses had to be replaced. In the second movie, I think we have five animatronic dinosaurs, and then on this movie, we had more than I could even count. Dozens! So in terms of how technology has changed, I've noticed there is more faith in some of the older practices and best practices that worked in the original *Jurassic Park*. I mean, honestly. You watch the original, and you're just like, "What?" So returning to that stuff is probably most thrilling to me.

Do you have a favorite *Dominion* memory?

Yes—I will never forget July 22 and July 23! It's when I filmed a sequence that you see in the trailer of me going underwater. It's a really fun sequence where I'm alone, and Colin, when we would talk about it, he would refer to it as my drum solo.

I've gotten to see the movie a couple times now, and whenever it gets to that section, it's so meaningful. It reminded me so much of the scene in the first one when I was running in heels and saying, "Open paddock 9!" Those were the physically hardest days on-set but also the most rewarding and the most fun, full-on action movie stuff. I'll never forget it.

> "ON THIS MOVIE, WE HAD MORE [ANIMATRONIC DINOSAURS] THAN I COULD EVEN COUNT"
> —*Bryce Dallas Howard*

RAMSAY COLE

Mamoudou Athie

Fans of indie films and Athie's captivating turn as Grandmaster Flash in Baz Luhrmann's Netflix series *The Get Down* may not recognize him as a biotech executive in *Jurassic World Dominion*, a project Athie called 'the most collaborative project I've ever worked on.' **BY BILL KEITH**

Do you remember getting the call for your first meeting?

I remember my agent called me while he was walking away from some studio lot and said, "Hey, Colin Trevorrow wants to meet with you on *Jurassic World*." It almost seemed like a joke to me, because I hadn't gotten anywhere close to anything like that. I emailed him later, and I was like, "Wait, so what were you talking about?" I ended up meeting with Colin somewhere in Malibu, we had like a three-hour very friendly, openhearted conversation over lobster rolls, and I was like, "Man, I got to work with this guy." Then, a couple months later, he called me to say I got the job. In a year I was on location.

What do you remember from your first day?

You have to remember, as a kid in my household, I saw this movie as a kid more than any other. So my first day was with Laura Dern and Sam Neill. I'm sitting with them in this helicopter like, "What the f---?" I mean, I don't really get starstruck, but it's *Jurassic Park*. It was just the craziest. I have never had a feeling like that on-set. It's making me laugh now because they're supercool, and it's not like they were being anything other than people. But for me, it was hard to separate for a little while.

What was shooting your first blockbuster like?

We're all living in this hotel together, so we really didn't interact with the world much outside of set and with COVID and the presidential election going on while we were there, it was a lot of, I think Patti Smith called it psychic nausea, but at the same time, we were having this strangely luxurious time in the countryside of England with, like, Laura Dern and Jeff Goldblum and Sam Neill, watching these guys' movies at the movie theater and just having chats about different things, getting advice, working out. It was this dichotomy of just insane stress and this very easy time. I got to know those guys pretty well, and I like them very, very, very much.

KAYLA WATTS DeWanda Wise

Director Colin Trevorrow didn't audition Wise as much as just talk to her about what kind of role she wanted. 'I have no idea what evidence he saw, but the man knows how to cast!' says Wise, who has gone on to star in the Netflix series reboot of Spike Lee's *She's Gotta Have It*. **BY BILL KEITH**

You first met with Colin in March of 2019. Do you remember much of what you discussed?

We talked about what it takes to build a cinematic icon. I consider myself as much a filmmaker as an actor, so I do have ideas, lots of ideas. But Colin's a boy from Oakland at the end of the day, so he was like, "What is this hair going to be?" That was the first question he asked me. And listen, she loves a hair story, you know?

What part of your own history did you bring to Kayla?

Colin and I essentially workshopped Kayla during my two weeks of quarantining when I first got to London, and I did a lot of the dialogue that ends up onscreen. I got to make her a multigenerational military woman. I'm from Maryland, and a lot of my family is like that, and I thought it would be dope if it was on her matriarchal side. If you saw Ketanji Brown Jackson's confirmation hearings, we made her like that—exceptionally resourceful and just crazy ready for anything.

What was your first day of actual shooting like?

It was the craziest, steepest learning curve. It's immensely technical, like stop-on-an-actual-dime-while-running kind of technical, and [Chris] Pratt has to be one of the world's most exceptional technicians. I would watch him watch his stunt double once and then be like, "Okay, got it." He's such a teacher. That first day, I was like, "Okay, cool. There's a lot of trust here, he's looking out for me, for my performance and for this character."

You worked with the original *Jurassic Park* actors Sam Neill, Laura Dern and Jeff Goldblum. Was that intimidating?

Whenever I get asked what it's like to work with all these icons, I'm always like, "By the time I got to work with them, they were my friends." We were together for so long before filming, so I wasn't on-set being like, "Oh my gosh, that's Laura Dern." I was like, "I braided her daughter's hair two months ago."

SURVIVING CAST

They've managed to avoid becoming raptor bait thus far. Here's who's returning from past films.

ZIA RODRIGUEZ
Daniella Pineda
The feisty and highly capable paleo vet has her hands full with many more patients.

DR. HENRY WU BD Wong
The brilliant geneticist has become aligned with darker forces, but he once worked next to John Hammond in *Jurassic Park*.

MAISIE LOCKWOOD
Isabella Sermon
Hammond's partner Lockwood's cloned granddaughter has much in common with the dinos.

FRANKLIN WEBB Justice Smith
The high-strung analyst for the Dinosaur Protection Group survived the rescue mission to Isla Nublar.

"IT'S GREAT TO BE BACK!"

Sam Neill, Laura Dern and Jeff Goldblum are back as the doctors Grant, Sattler and Malcolm, in roles that director Colin Trevorrow says has them on 'equal footing with all the *Jurassic World* characters.' **BY BILL KEITH**

WHEN *DOMINION* WRITER-DIRECTOR COLIN Trevorrow set about including original *Jurassic Park* stars Laura Dern, Jeff Goldblum and Sam Neill in a sequel, he was faced with the most difficult challenges that had nothing to do with Hollywood deal-making.

"It was about storytelling," he says. "The reason why Laura, Sam and Jeff's characters weren't in the first two movies is that I didn't really have a logical way to bring them into the world that we had built without it seeming like a couple of writers trying to figure out how to bring legacy characters into a movie."

Steven Spielberg began building his original team in 1992. At the time, 40-year-old Jeff Goldblum's performance in *The Fly* was still so indelible that *Jurassic Park*'s casting agent Janet Hirshenson could only see him as Ian Malcolm after reading the script Michael Crichton had adapted from his bestselling novel; Laura Dern was 25, fresh off her first Oscar nomination for *Rambling Rose*, and had agreed to audition for the "dinosaur movie" at the urging of her *Wild at Heart* costar Nicolas Cage; and Sam Neill, 44, was on his way to a job in Canada when he got a call from his agent saying he had 30 minutes to meet with Spielberg, who had liked his performance in *Dead Calm*. (He immediately hopped in a cab to the director's house.)

Just four weeks later, the trio was in Hawaii to start shooting. As Goldblum

▲ The legacy cast returns in *Jurassic World Dominion*. Far left: Dr. Ellie Sattler (Laura Dern) and Dr. Alan Grant (Sam Neill); above: Dr. Ian Malcolm (Jeff Goldblum).

◀ The cast in *Jurassic Park*.

> **"THE DINOSAURS FEEL MORE REAL THAN EVER FOR ME... COLIN DESIGNED IT SO THAT WE COULD HAVE AS MANY REAL DINOSAURS ACTING WITH US AS POSSIBLE INSTEAD OF CGI STUFF"**
>
> *–Jeff Goldblum*

remembers it, they got to the set without much prep at all: "We didn't have any rehearsal or table read or anything like that. We showed up in Kauai, and I don't think I even saw Steven in the hotel. We just all got a ride to set together, me and Sam and Laura in a Jeep," he says.

Spielberg was counting on his actors performing while awestruck by the enormous $63 million budget. "When we got there, [Steven] said, 'I don't want to rehearse or even block this for camera. I think we should get a skeletal idea then turn on the juice. Because if it works out, it's going to have something fresh about it that I don't want to have to put in Tupperware and re-create in some way, even if it's 10 minutes later.' And that's what we started to do."

In the intervening years, the original film went on to win three Oscars and, after its triumphant 2013 3-D rerelease, earn more than $1 billion at the box office. The actors have collected Oscar and Emmy nominations as well as an Academy Award win for Dern following 2019's *Marriage Story*. So nearly three decades later, when Trevorrow gathered the legacy cast together for a Zoom call, the director was the one in awe.

"I remember being on there with Sam, Laura and Jeff, and then the fourth box was me," Trevorrow recalls. "It was the strangest Brady Bunch, but we managed to pull it off."

It wasn't his first interaction with the three, of course. Long before that call, Trevorrow had met with each of the actors to discuss where he had hoped to take each of their characters—and to ask for input from each.

Trevorrow and Goldblum had briefly worked together for his appearance in *Fallen Kingdom* and then again on a Super Bowl commercial. "We did this Jeep commercial and even then I told him that I planned for him to come back," the director says. "Sam Neill and I sat down and had a lunch together in one of those moments that a lot of directors have to face, where you're sitting across from a legend and you have to somehow convince someone who's used to working with Steven Spielberg that, 'Well, Mr. Spielberg isn't available right now, so you're going to get me,'" he says.

He had a similar moment with Laura. "I came in with great reverence and great respect," says Trevorrow. His goal was to "not just trot out these characters for the sake of having them in the movie. I wanted them on equal footing with all the *Jurassic World* characters." Or as Neill puts it: "He was anxious to assure us that

▲ From left: Goldblum, Dern and Neill. The three have not been in a film together since *Jurassic Park* in 1993.

we wouldn't just be there in a cameo…and that even at my age, we would be required to hurtle around doing Jurassic things, so that was cool."

The legacy actors were thrilled by the opportunity to be more than just nostalgic set dressing and (literally in some cases) leaped at the chance to settle scores for their iconic characters. For his part, Goldblum was eager to bounce back after getting memorably sidelined by a T. rex in his first appearance. "I was plenty satisfied with the physical action that I had in this one," he says. "I like how Colin and everybody rose to the challenge of giving us something satisfying to do with each other. It was thrilling to work with Sam and Laura again, and, of course, with so many great new people, it was just spectacular."

Neill and Dern's Alan and Ellie had some unfinished business too. "It was great to be back with some old friends and make some new ones at the same time. Alan is still a crusty old bachelor," says Neill. "Then the love of his life turns up and one way or another he finds himself having to be responsible for looking after a kid. Life can be funny that way."

And what of their nonhuman costars? "They made so many big breakthroughs for the original, special effects-wise, and it's been evolving ever since, so it still feels like a new kind of enhanced version of what's ever been done before," says Goldblum. "The dinosaurs feel more real than ever for me, and that's kind of spectacular because I know that Colin designed it so that we could have as many real dinosaurs acting with us as possible instead of CGI stuff."

In the end, Trevorrow hopes he's successfully completed his most important task: earning the return of the legendary stars in a way that makes sense to the franchise's core DNA. "Finally in this third movie, we found a way for it to make some fundamental sense for them to be there, that now is the moment when they would have something to say," he says. "I hope that everybody walks away feeling that it wouldn't have worked exactly the way it works without them."

Our No. 8 pick: Tim (Joseph Mazzello) hides from two raptors in *Jurassic Park*.

Top 12 Beastly Moments

EVER SINCE *JURASSIC PARK* ROARED INTO THEATERS, THE BLOCKBUSTER FILMS HAVE CONSISTENTLY DELIVERED FANTASTIC THRILLS. HERE, OUR PICKS FOR THE 12 MOST UNFORGETTABLE SCENES. *By Sean Smith and Gina McIntyre*

LIFE, UH, FINDS A WAY
Jurassic Park (1993)

The Jurassic movies aren't exactly known for their dialogue, and this scene, set in the first 35 minutes of the first movie, doesn't include a single dinosaur or DNA strand of action, but it has shaped the entire franchise more than any other. As chaos theorist Dr. Ian Malcolm (Jeff Goldblum) is told by John Hammond (Richard Attenborough) and Dr. Henry Wu (BD Wong) that the dinosaurs will never be able to breed because they're all female, and that these prehistoric behemoths can be controlled, he issues a warning that will go on to become the moral and philosophical touchstone of the entire franchise. "Life will not be contained. Life breaks free," he says. "Life, uh, finds a way." Now, three decades years later, it's still the most memorable line of the franchise.

FEELING BLUE
Jurassic World (2015)

Loyalty counts in the Jurassic movies, and for the first time in the series that rule extends to the dinosaurs themselves. In the film's climactic scene, Indominus rex is about to destroy a T. rex—and then every living thing on the island—when Blue, the velociraptor raised from birth by Owen Grady (Chris Pratt), comes to the rescue, jumping onto Indominus's back and distracting her long enough for the T. rex to rejoin the fight. In a final face-off, Blue and the T. rex force Indominus against the sea wall, where the monster is snatched into the sea by the Mosasaurus. Blue shares a final look with Grady before trotting off to freedom. Interspecies love never felt so good.

NO WONDER YOU'RE EXTINCT
Jurassic Park (1993)

Ah, sweet justice! In the Jurassic franchise, the bad guys with the least respect for the animals often get their just deserts—or rather, become desserts. The first delicious casualty is disgruntled computer programmer Dennis Nedry (Wayne Knight), who sabotages the park's facilities as part of his plan to steal dino embryos. In his escape, though, his Jeep gets caught in a mud bank, where he's confronted by a chirpy little Dilophosaurus. He tries to shoo it away, but when it fails to obey, he barks, "No wonder you're extinct." Don't diss the dino, dude. Seconds later, the Dilo unfurls its giant cowl, blinds him with poison saliva and . . . just like that, a yummy sleazebag sundae!

11

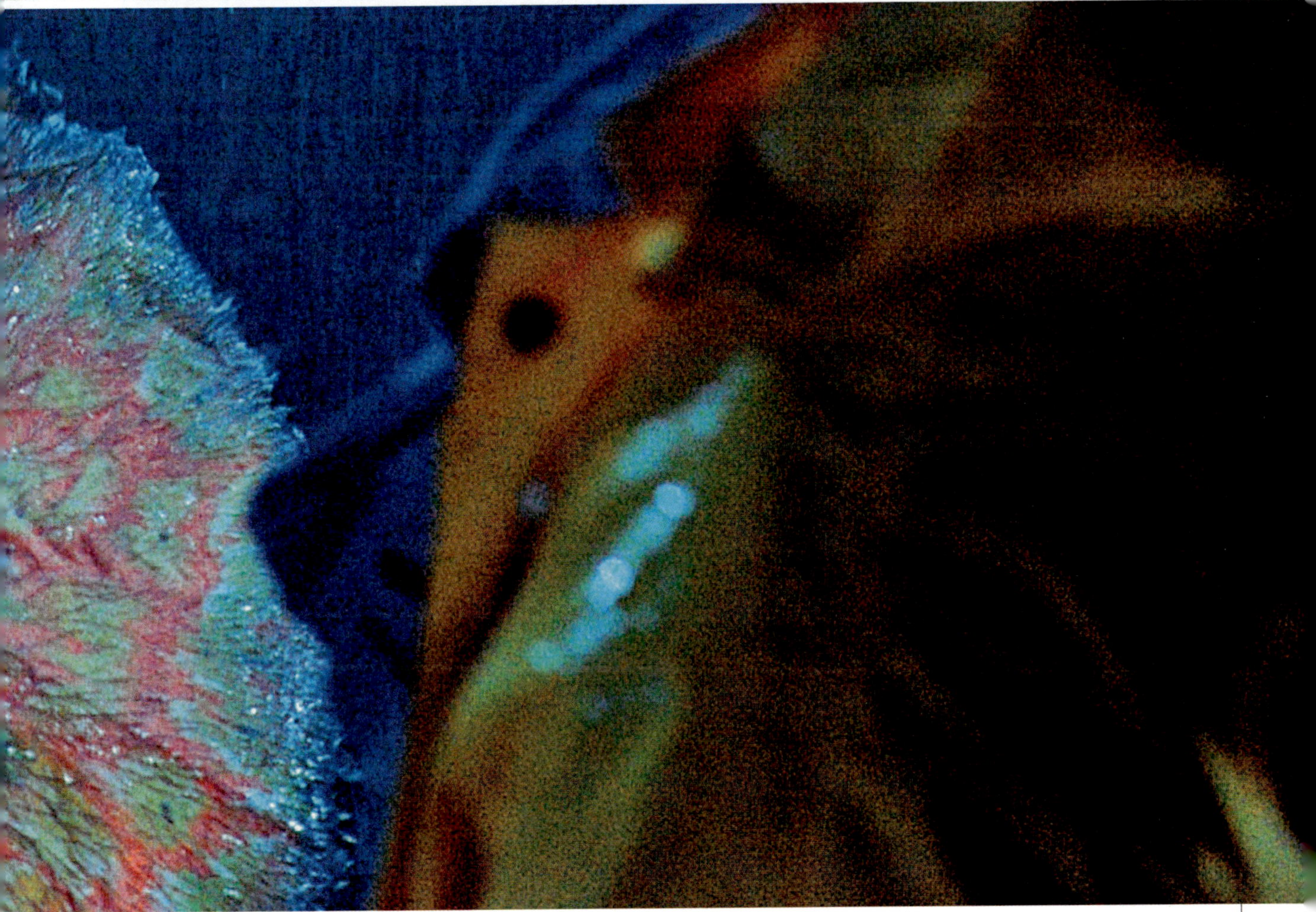

9 T-REX AND GYRO
Fallen Kingdom (2018)

Spectacle just doesn't come much bigger than this key set-piece from *Fallen Kingdom*. As raptor trainer Owen and animal activists Claire (Bryce Dallas Howard) and Franklin (Justice Smith) are fleeing the volcanic eruption that threatens to destroy Isla Nublar, they discover an empty gyrosphere, which just might ferry them to safety. But before Owen can join his friends inside the transport, the trio is threatened by a hungry Carnotaurus—only to watch in shock (and relief?) as the dinosaur is easily taken down by a T. rex. The mighty creature throws back its head to roar in victory as an explosive cloud consumes the landscape.

8 WHAT'S FOR DINNER?
Jurassic Park (1993)

Kids-in-peril scenes have become a hallmark of the franchise, and it all started here, with siblings Lex (Ariana Richards) and Tim (Joseph Mazzello) hiding in Jurassic Park's industrial kitchen from two velociraptors. The kids scamper along the floor as the raptors open doors (!), knock over pans with their tails, sniff ladles and generally menace them before one, at least, is tricked by a reflection in a stainless-steel cabinet. The kids lock it inside a walk-in cooler and escape before becoming tartare tapas.

9

7

WE'RE GOING TO NEED A BIGGER T. REX
Jurassic Park III (2001)

After reigning as the queen of the jungle in the first two films, the T. rex discovers that no one stays on top forever. In the franchise's first major dino vs. dino fight scene, Rex battles to the death with a massive ridge-backed Spinosaurus aegyptiacus and loses when the Spino snaps her neck. Pity. We were finally starting to like her.

6

MEET THE NEW POOL BOY
The Lost World: Jurassic Park (1997)

Amid all the screaming, there are also times to laugh, and Steven Spielberg obliges with this comic-relief gem. As a papa T. rex terrorizes San Diego in the middle of the night, a boy wakes up to see it drinking from his family's backyard pool. He rouses his parents, who naturally don't believe him—until they look out his window. In a classic three-shot, the kid, as his parents scream in horror, calmly snaps a photo. Picture-perfect.

5

GOT YOUR GOAT
Jurassic Park (1993)

Steven Spielberg brilliantly hides the T. rex until the film's halfway point and then delivers in gory cinematic glory with this scene that starts in a tropical storm with a live goat hors d'oeuvre and ends with screaming kids in a Jeep and a smarmy InGen lawyer (Martin Ferrero) being chomped, head first, while he cowers on a toilet. No movie monster has ever made a more terrifying entrance.

5

4

4

INDO STALKS MAISIE
Fallen Kingdom (2018)

Director J.A. Bayona channels his considerable facility for horror movie thrills into an unforgettable sequence in which the predatory Indoraptor stalks Maisie (Isabella Sermon) through the Lockwood estate. As the child lies shivering in terror under the covers of her bed, the bloodthirsty creature steals into the room and advances menacingly toward its trembling prey. As it claws and teeth edge closer to her tiny face, she screams. Sure, it's the stuff of nightmares, but it's all staged so gorgeously that it's impossible to look away.

3

PEOPLE IN GLASS HOUSES...
The Lost World: Jurassic Park (1997)

"Mommy's very angry," Malcolm says. Yep. So is Daddy. When Dr. Sarah Harding (Julianne Moore) and Nick Van Owen (Vince Vaughn) rush an injured baby T. rex back to their high-tech trailer on the edge of a cliff for medical attention, the kid's parents are not pleased. In a white-knuckle sequence, the beasts push the trailer over the cliff. Harding plummets onto a window high above the ocean. As she tries to move, spider veins in the glass snap and crack around her, while Malcolm, Van Owen and, above on land, Eddie Carr (Richard Schiff) try to save her—and themselves—before the trailer crashes into the water. Oh, and did we mention that it's nighttime and pouring rain? If you weren't already terrified of heights (or T. rexes), this should fix that.

SIZE MATTERS

We measure the average size* of the most notable dinosaurs pictured in their years of screen fame.

*as shown in the Jurassic films

COMPSOGNATHUS
16 in. tall
30 in. long
12 lbs.

DIMORPHODON
3.3 ft. tall
8 ft. long
4 lbs.

VELOCIRAPTOR
5.6 ft. tall
15 ft. long
300 lbs.

GALLIMIMUS
6.3 ft. tall
20 ft. long
950 lbs.

ANKYLOSAURUS
5.6 ft. tall
35 ft. long
6.5 tons

DILOPHOSAURUS
8 ft. tall
20 ft. long
1,000 lbs.

PTERANODON
9.5 ft. tall
18 ft. long
70 lbs.

STEGOSAURUS
9 ft. tall
28 ft. long
6 tons

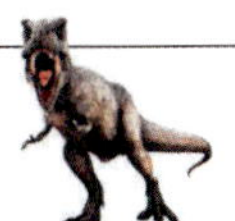

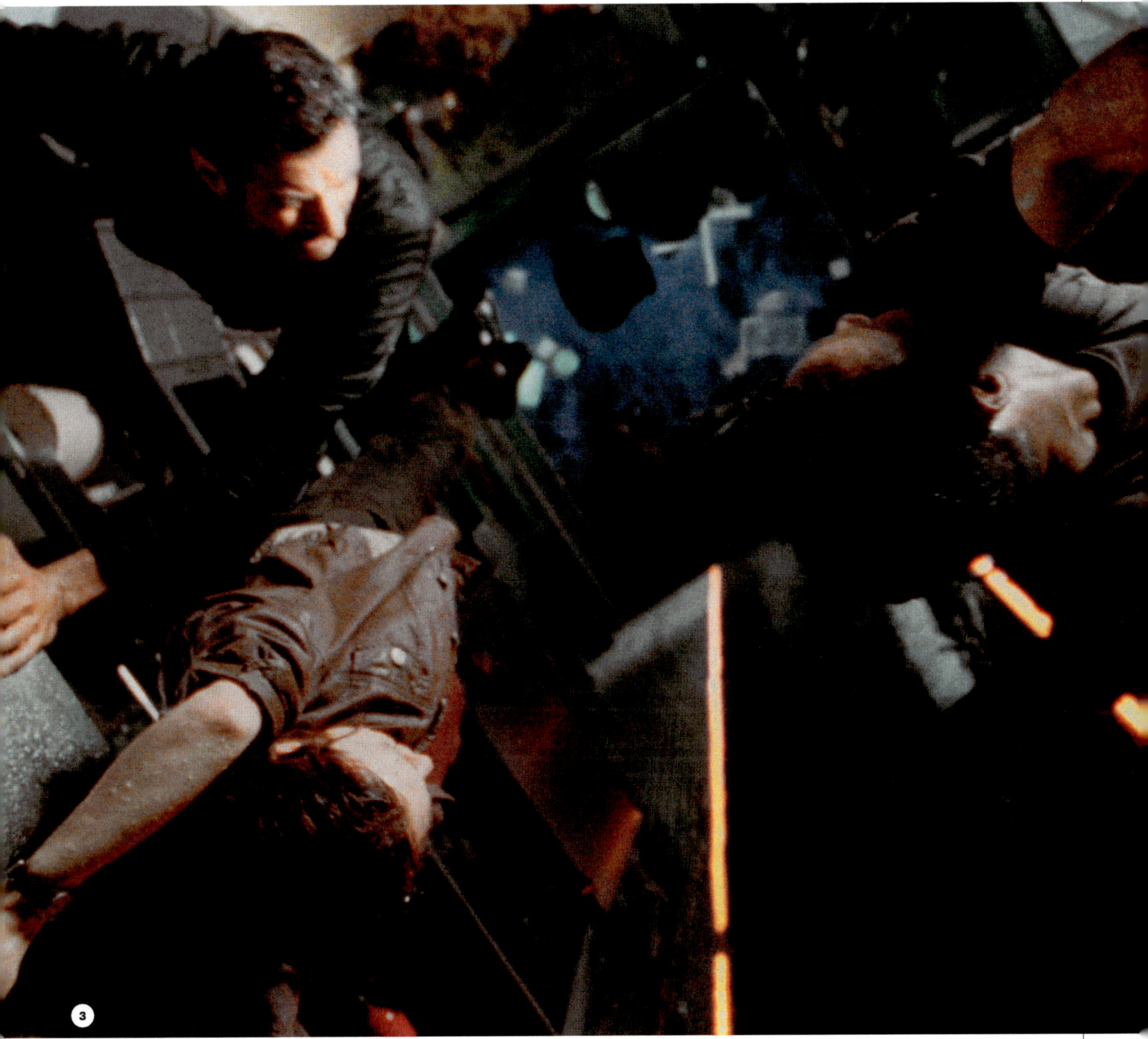

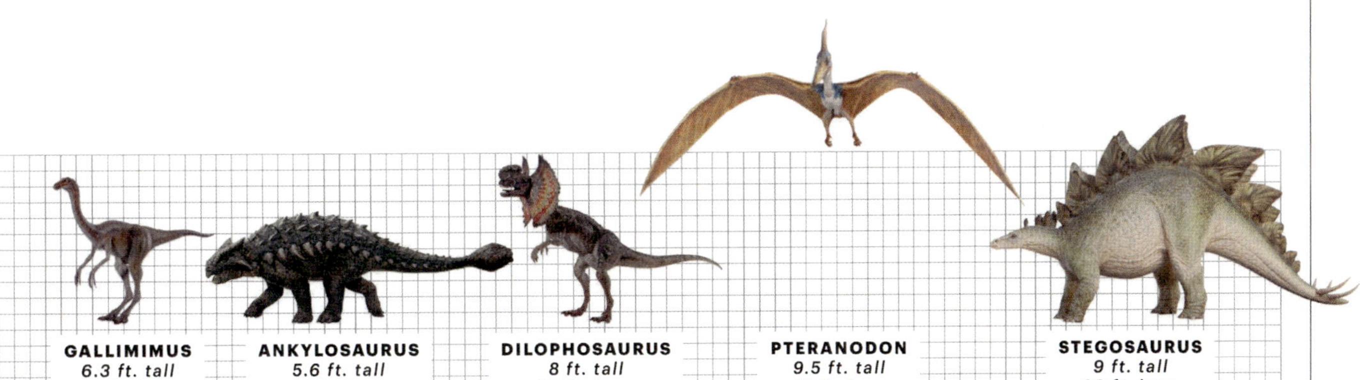

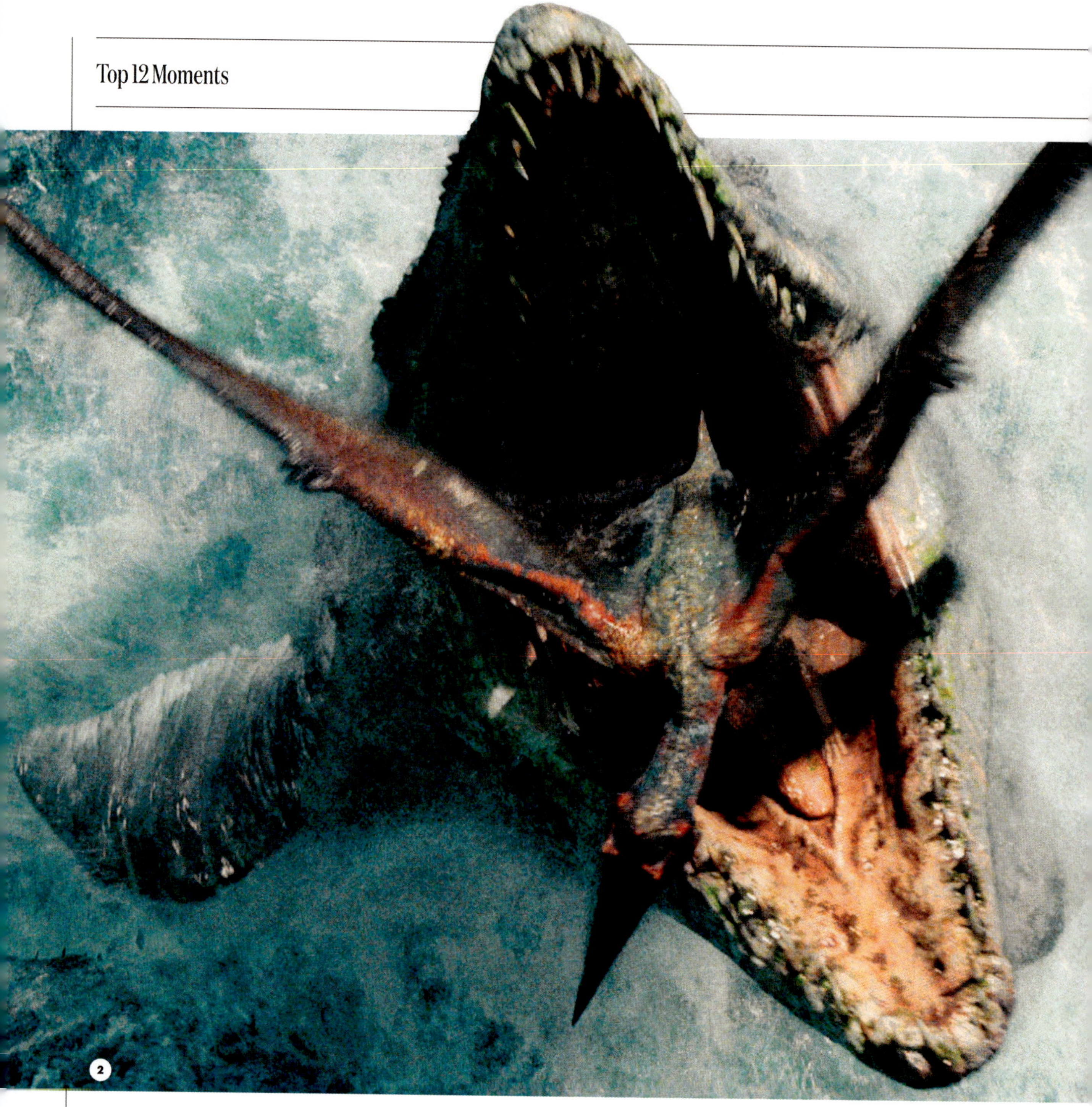
2

TRICERATOPS
9.8 ft. tall
25.5 ft. long
12 tons
PARASAUROLOPHUS
9 ft. tall
40 ft. long
2 tons
PACHYCEPHALOSAURUS
17.5 ft. tall
16 ft. long
1,000 lbs.
TYRANNOSAURUS REX
20 ft. tall
40 ft. long
9 tons

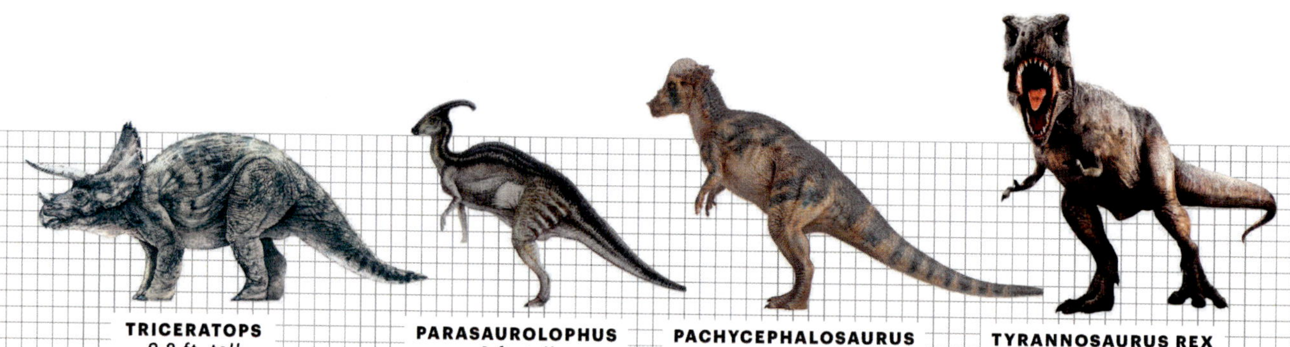

2

THE FLIGHT OF ZARA
Jurassic World (2015)

The world's unluckiest assistant, Zara (Katie McGrath), is tasked by Claire Dearing (Bryce Dallas Howard) with babysitting Dearing's nephews (Nick Robinson and Ty Simpkins) as they tour Jurassic World. She's rewarded for her efforts by being snatched from the park's Main Street by a flying pteranodon, dropped into the tank, grabbed underwater again by the ptera and lifted into the air before both she and the ptera are gulped down by the massive sea dinosaur the Mosasaurus. Worst job ever? Def. But possibly the franchise's coolest death.

1

WELCOME TO JURASSIC PARK
Jurassic Park (1993)

For all the jaw-dropping moments in this franchise, nothing can top the first time we all saw a living dinosaur. As John Hammond gives his visitors their first glimpse at the reptiles he has resurrected from extinction, they, and we, gaze up in wonder at a towering Brachiosaurus.
"You did it, you crazy sonofabitch. You did it," Malcolm says. Exactly.

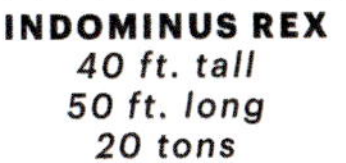

"I thought the T. rex was one of the most awesome dinosaurs," says Steven Spielberg.

JURASSIC PARK

The Complete Oral History

THE YEAR WAS 1993, AND *JURASSIC PARK* WAS SCARING THE BEJESUS OUT OF MOVIEGOERS EVERYWHERE. IN 2013 *EW* GATHERED STEVEN SPIELBERG AND THE CAST AND CREW TOGETHER TO RELIVE THE MAKING OF A MEGAHIT THAT SPAWNED A DIGITAL REVOLUTION. *By Tim Stack and Keith Staskiewicz*

JURASSIC PARK 1993

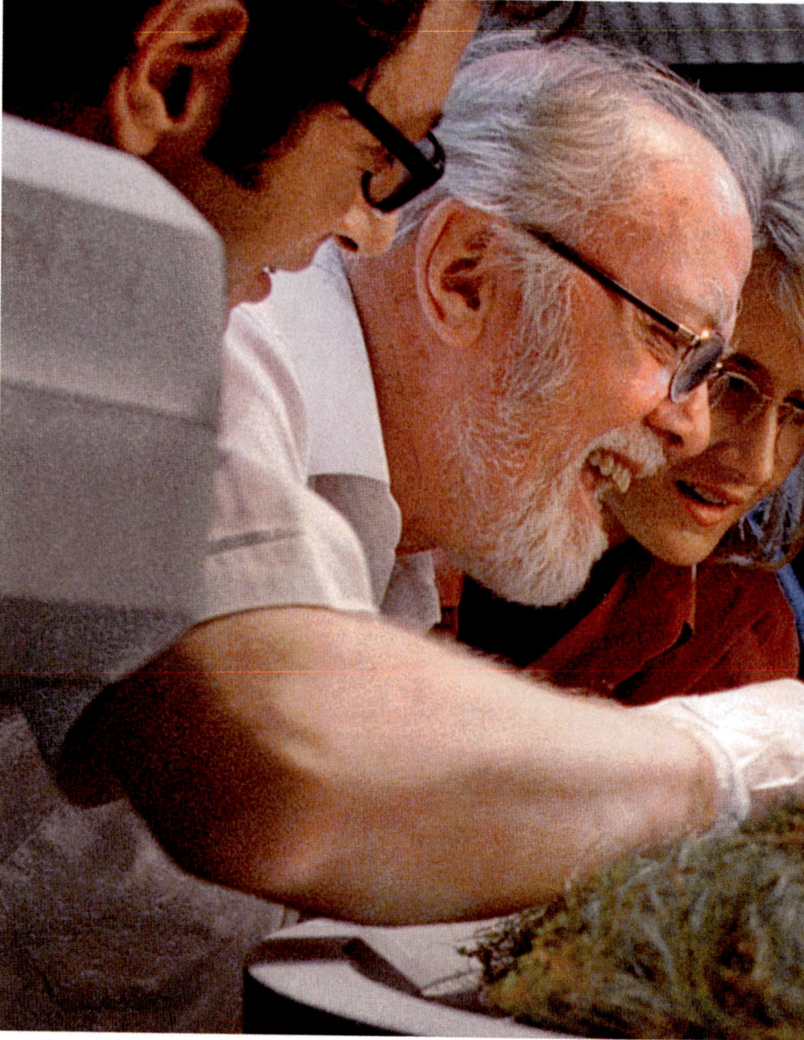

STEVEN SPIELBERG AND AUTHOR MICHAEL Crichton had been meeting about developing a feature based on Crichton's script *Cold Case,* about his time as a medical resident. (Later, it would become the TV series *ER.*) Crichton, who died from cancer in 2008, mentioned another idea he was working on: a novel about dinosaurs being brought back to life through old samples of their DNA.

Spielberg was immediately hooked. When galleys for *Jurassic Park* made their way around Hollywood in May 1990, the sci-fi adventure became the "it" project to buy. According to Spielberg, other interested directors might have included Richard Donner (*Lethal Weapon*) and James Cameron (*Avatar*). Universal won the bidding war, thanks in large part to Spielberg's relationship with Crichton.

The director started storyboarding before the script was even written and quickly assembled an effects team. Creature master Stan Winston (*Aliens*) created the large-form models, including a nearly 20-ft.-tall T. rex, and stop-motion artist Phil Tippett (*RoboCop*) would animate miniatures based on those Winston designs for the more elaborate action sequences. Then Industrial Light & Magic's Dennis Muren, who had just designed the liquid-metal effects in *Terminator 2: Judgment Day,* brought up the idea of using CGI to animate the dinosaurs. Muren invited Spielberg, producer Kathleen Kennedy and Tippett to watch a CG demo of a Gallimimus stampede.

STEVEN SPIELBERG *Director* Here's what was scary: We were creating the title characters of a film. These were the stars of the picture, these dinosaurs. And if that didn't work, nothing about *Jurassic Park* could have worked. So that was daunting, because I was using Universal's money to basically make an experimental dinosaur picture.

KATHLEEN KENNEDY *Producer* I remember getting the phone call where Dennis said, "I think I have something you and Steven should take a look at." We saw this wire-frame model of a dinosaur running across the screen, and it caused five or six of us to literally leap to our feet because it was so extraordinary and significantly beyond anything we had seen in motion control up to that point.

SPIELBERG The last time my jaw dropped like that was when George Lucas showed me the shot of the Imperial cruiser [in *Star Wars*]. I showed it to [stop-motion-effects legend] Ray Harryhausen. He was absolutely enthralled and very positive about the paradigm changing. He looked at the test and said, "Well, that's the future."

DENNIS MUREN *Full-Motion Dinosaurs* I knew how hard it was to get these effects to look good, and I was just sitting there saying, "This is impossible that we did it." Since the early '80s there was this

> “IT CHANGED SPECIAL EFFECTS FOREVER, AND FOR BETTER OR FOR WORSE, IT REALLY DID INTRODUCE THE DIGITAL ERA”
>
> *–Director Steven Spielberg*

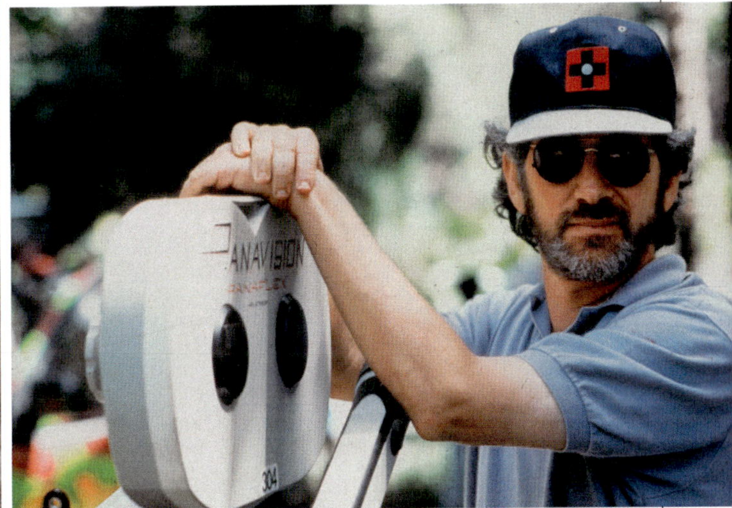

▲ From left: Jeff Goldblum (Dr. Ian Malcolm), Richard Attenborough (John Hammond), Laura Dern (Dr. Ellie Sattler), Sam Neill (Dr. Alan Grant) and BD Wong (Dr. Henry Wu).

▲ As a child, Spielberg was fascinated by dinosaurs. "I was more interested in the dinosaurs in [1933's] *King Kong* than I was in King Kong himself," remembers the director.

◀ Dr. Sattler, Tim (Joseph Mazzello) and Dr. Grant inspect a Triceratops. The dinosaur was one of many full-size puppets created by Stan Winston's team for *Jurassic Park*.

promise that CGI could do this, and it had finally delivered.

PHIL TIPPETT *Dinosaur Supervisor* Steven asked me how I felt after seeing the footage, and I said, "I think I'm extinct." He said, "That's a great line. I'm putting that in the movie."

Although his go-motion models were not used in the film, Tippett, a paleontology enthusiast, ended up staying on as a sort of choreographer for the dinosaurs. He even insisted the animators take mime classes over the course of six weeks to learn how to move like a dinosaur.

TIPPETT It's very helpful physically. When you act it out, you internalize it. You can feel it a different way.

SPIELBERG Phil gave all the dinosaurs personalities and real characteristics based on his experience with the animal kingdom and the natural world.

TIPPETT Another thing that was really important is that they locked me in a room with Gary Rydstrom for a week. Before we started doing the actual performances, I wanted to have the dinosaur voices, or as close as we could.

GARY RYDSTROM *Sound Designer* I tried to stay organic, so all the dinosaur stuff is from real animals. The raptor is probably made up of bits and pieces of 20 or 30 different animals, to make a vocabulary. So breathing, guttural sounds, screams, communication—that kind of thing. But the main attack scream is a combination of a walrus, for the low frequency, and then the higher-frequency range was a boy dolphin pining for a female.

With preproduction underway, Spielberg selected screenwriter David Koepp to help Crichton adapt the book, based on a recommendation from Robert Zemeckis, who was directing *Death Becomes Her*, cowritten by Koepp. Spielberg then set about finding the actors who would spend much of their screen time running from these ancient behemoths, including director Richard Attenborough as park creator John Hammond; Jeff Goldblum as chaos (and quip) expert Ian Malcolm; Sam Neill as stern Dr. Alan Grant; and Ariana Richards and Joseph Mazzello as Hammond's grandkids. Laura Dern was Spielberg's first choice to play paleobotanist Dr. Ellie Sattler.

LAURA DERN *Dr. Ellie Sattler* I was talking with Nicolas Cage, and we had just done *Wild at Heart* together, and I said to him, "Nic, they want to put me on the phone with Steven Spielberg, but they want to talk to me about a dinosaur movie...." And he was like, "You are *doing* a dinosaur movie! No one can ever say no to a dinosaur movie!" I was like, "Really?" And he's like, "Are you kidding? It's a dream of my life to do a movie with dinosaurs!" [*Laughs*] So he was such an influence on me. Then I talked to Steven, and he goes, "I know that you're doing your independent films, but I need you to be chased by dinosaurs, in awe of dinosaurs, and have the adventure of a lifetime. Will you do this with me?" And I was like, "Sure."

ARIANA RICHARDS *Lex* I was called into a casting office, and they just wanted me to scream. I heard later on that Steven had watched a few girls on tape that day, and I was the only one who ended up waking his sleeping wife off the couch, and she came running through the hallway to see if the kids were all right.

JOSEPH MAZZELLO *Tim* Steven had me screen-test with Robin Williams and Dustin Hoffman for *Hook*. I was just too young for the role. And because of that, Steven came up to me and said, "Don't worry about it, Joey. I'm going to get you in a movie this summer." Not only a nice

◀ Stan Winston and his team prepare for the T. rex night scene. On-set the puppet's foam skin absorbed the water, making the dino hard to handle.

▼ Top: Grant distracts the dinosaur; the creature was digitally inserted into the shot. Bottom: Sattler and Muldoon (Bob Peck) discover Malcolm injured in the road.

> "THE THING WAS BREATHING – STAN WINSTON'S PUPPETS WERE SO INCREDIBLE. TO TOUCH THEM WAS TO BLOW YOUR MIND"
>
> *–Sam Neill*

promise to get, but to have it be one of the biggest box office smashes of all time? That's a pretty good trade.

THE PRODUCTION

Filming began in August 1992 on Kauai, Hawaii. Sometimes the actors had to react to a crudely drawn T. rex head on a stick (with digital effects added later), but other times they got to face off against Winston's life-size creations.

DERN When I saw the Triceratops, I couldn't believe it. Neither could Sam Neill—we were both freaking out. And like Sam does in the movie, we did lay ourselves over the belly and feel the belly moving in and out. I forced my way in, and [the puppeteers] let me go into the belly of the dinosaur and watch them work.

SAM NEILL *Dr. Alan Grant* The thing was breathing—Stan Winston's puppets were so incredible. To touch them was to blow your mind.

Everything went smoothly until the last day of shooting. Spielberg awoke in his hotel room at 4 a.m. and noticed the staff bringing in all of the pool chairs. In a few hours Hurricane Iniki—the most powerful storm on record to hit Hawaii—would strike.

SPIELBERG I turned on the TV. There was an animation of the Hawaiian island chain. The island we were on, Kauai, was outlined in red, and there was a big arrow pointing to it, and then there was the icon of a cyclonic hurricane moving directly toward us. It was like a movie.

NEILL We were all huddled into the ballroom of this hotel, which was completely trashed in the course of the hurricane. What kept morale up was that the only thing to read in the whole ballroom, the only thing anyone thought to bring in with them, was a Victoria's Secret catalog. So that, in our darkest moments, cheered us up.

JEFF GOLDBLUM *Ian Malcolm* The lights went out, and I remember Steven Spielberg took a flashlight and held it above his head and shined it down on himself and said, "Love story," and then put it under his chin and said, "Horror story. Love story. Horror story."

Once the storm passed, the cast and crew were airlifted out of Hawaii and returned to L.A. to shoot the remainder of the film, including the most iconic action sequence: the T. rex's attack on Dr. Grant and the kids in their Ford Explorer. Spielberg had storyboarded extensively and even enlisted Tippett to create a mini stop-motion animation of the pivotal moment. But as Goldblum's Malcolm implies in the film, not everything can be predicted.

SPIELBERG I was listening to Earth, Wind & Fire [in my car] and had it cranked up really loud. I suddenly saw my rearview mirror vibrating every time the horns section came in. I thought, "What if when the T. rex approaches, the mirror starts vibrating?" That is in the picture. But then I thought, "What if it was a glass of water and these concentric circles?" So I gave it to Michael Lantieri, the guy in charge of physical effects, and he came up with how to actually achieve those ripples by using guitar strings [placed under the dashboard].

JOHN ROSENGRANT *Stan Winston Studio Puppeteer* The T. rex was 36 feet long and 18 feet tall. We're talking about a hydraulically powered creature that felt like a bus going by you when it would move. We found out not long before we were going to shoot that it was going to be raining [in

▲
Left: Spielberg (at far right) with the cast. Right: Grant flees from a herd of Gallimimus.

▶
Grant, Lex and Tim observe the Brachiosaurus (or, as Tim calls them, "Veggiesaurus") eat. In this particular frame, the dinos were digitally created, but Winston's team created the neck and head of one of the creatures (see page 52).

the scene]. So it went from this beautifully tuned machine that worked fantastically to... suddenly the foam-rubber skin started absorbing water, and now all of the calculations were off, and it started to shudder. We went out and bought tons of towels and started putting big blowers, dryers, on it to dry it out.

KENNEDY The T. rex went into the heebie-jeebies sometimes. Scared the crap out of us. We'd be, like, eating lunch, and all of a sudden a T. rex would come alive. At first we didn't know what was happening, and then we realized it was the rain. You'd hear people start screaming.

MAZZELLO We were in that car, and I think the T. rex was only supposed to go down so far, and the Plexiglas was the only thing between the dinosaur and us. It came down too far one time, and it chipped the Plexiglas and broke a tooth. And if you pause on it, you can actually see in the movie that there's a shot during that scene where the T. rex was missing a tooth.

NEILL I've still got a big scar on my left hand that I'm looking at right now from the flare. It dropped some burning phosphorous on me and got under my watch and took a chunk of my arm out.

THE PHENOMENON

Jurassic Park wrapped 12 days ahead of schedule. Kennedy and George Lucas oversaw postproduction while Spielberg was in Europe shooting *Schindler's List.* The film opened on Friday, June 11, 1993, and broke box office records its first weekend, with $47 million. It eventually went on to make more than $1 billion worldwide.

DAVID KOEPP *Screenwriter* I remember the day it opened I was in New York, and I walked to the Ziegfeld [Theatre] to see how it was doing. The guy comes out and announces to the big line, "Ladies and gentlemen, the 7 o'clock show of *Jurassic Park* is sold out." And people go, "Oooh." And he goes, "Also the 10 o'clock show is sold out." And they went, "Ooooooh." "And also Saturday night's 7 and 10 o'clock shows are also sold out." And I was like, "I'm not an expert, but I think this is very good."

SPIELBERG My reaction was "Thank God." I don't often preview the movies I direct. I did not preview *Jurassic Park.* The first time I saw it was at a theater with the 8 p.m. Friday audience. I sat in the back with my agent Mike Ovitz and my wife.

KENNEDY That was a period of time when it was so fun to release movies because it was like a rock concert. You'd get in a limo and get a couple bottles of champagne and drive around town and see the lines around the block and people going crazy and getting dressed up. And then you go into the theater, and people were so excited. We've lost a bit of that with movies opening in so many theaters.

MAZZELLO It was wild. I couldn't leave the house. I would be walking down the street, and I would get mobbed.

DERN [People were like,] "Oh my gosh, you're the girl who put your hand in the dinosaur poo!" That was my big entrée. I have met kids who were afraid to shake my hand, as though I hadn't washed.

KENNEDY In many ways it's one of Steven's really great movies. When you look at what the technology spawned, it's pretty remarkable what a game changer it was.

SPIELBERG I think people like *Jurassic Park* because it's a helluva yarn.

◀
The final shot of dinosaurs in *Jurassic Park* was, naturally, a T. rex-velociraptor battle.

▼
Left: Ariana Richards's Lex as she realizes a raptor has made its way into the dining hall. Right: Spielberg directs that scene, in which one of the dinosaurs appears behind a curtain in back of Joseph Mazzello's Tim.

MAPPING THE PARK

Built on a tropical island and dreamed up by the eccentric Dr. Hammond (Richard Attenborough), Isla Nublar is the setting for *Jurassic Park* and two of its sequels. Here are some of the key spots you should know. **BY SEAN SMITH**

1. VISITORS CENTER

Oh, it all seems so wondrous at first! The main reception and dining hall in Jurassic Park welcomes visitors to a world beyond the imagination, with a spectacular T. rex skeleton in the place of honor. The resort showplace will later become a refuge of last resort, with Dr. Hammond's grandchildren attempting to hide from velociraptors in the kitchen and the surviving adults facing the final battle of human versus reptile.

2. THE GREAT LAWN

As our team of intrepid scientists emerges from the jungle into a green pasture, Dr. Alan Grant (Sam Neill), Dr. Ellie Sattler (Laura Dern) and Dr. Ian Malcolm (Jeff Goldblum) get their first glimpse of a living, breathing dinosaur: a towering Brachiosaurus. This location will remain an area of wonder (and one stampede) throughout the franchise until it becomes the site of slaughter in *Jurassic World*, when an Indominus rex begins killing other dinosaurs for sport.

4. T. REX PEN

The Tyrannosaurus rex plays possum for the first half of the film before showing up in a rainstorm, with the power out, to devour a goat, break through a fence, snatch a skeezy lawyer off the john and terrorize two adorable children. It's the site of the most dramatic entrance in the franchise's history.

3. CAGED DINO

In *Jurassic Park* Dr. Hammond hopes to wow his guests and his grandchildren with the first automated Jeep tour through the park. Their first stop, at the Dilophosaurus pen, is a bit of a bust, though, as the poisonous hooded creatures fail to emerge. They do show up later, however, when one kills computer-tech-on-the-lam Dennis Nedry (Wayne Knight).

The 20-ft.-tall, 13,000-lb. mechanical T. rex proved terrifying on the big screen.

SPECIAL EFFECTS

Building *a* Better Dinosaur

THE GAME-CHANGING CINEMATIC ACHIEVEMENTS OF *JURASSIC PARK*'S F/X TEAMS WERE NEARLY AS ASTOUNDING AS THE ADVANCES OF JOHN HAMMOND'S GENETIC SCIENTISTS. *By Jeff Labrecque*

FACE TO FACE

Initially Steven Spielberg intended for all of his dinosaurs to be full-size robotic creatures. That led him to Stan Winston (above), the creature F/X magician who had worked with James Cameron on *Aliens* and *Terminator 2*. Even after Spielberg shifted tack and decided to rely more heavily on groundbreaking computer-generated dinosaurs, he leaned on Winston's team to construct convincing life-size animatronic heads and torsos, like the T. rex and this Brachiosaurus, in order for them "to act" on-camera opposite the human characters.

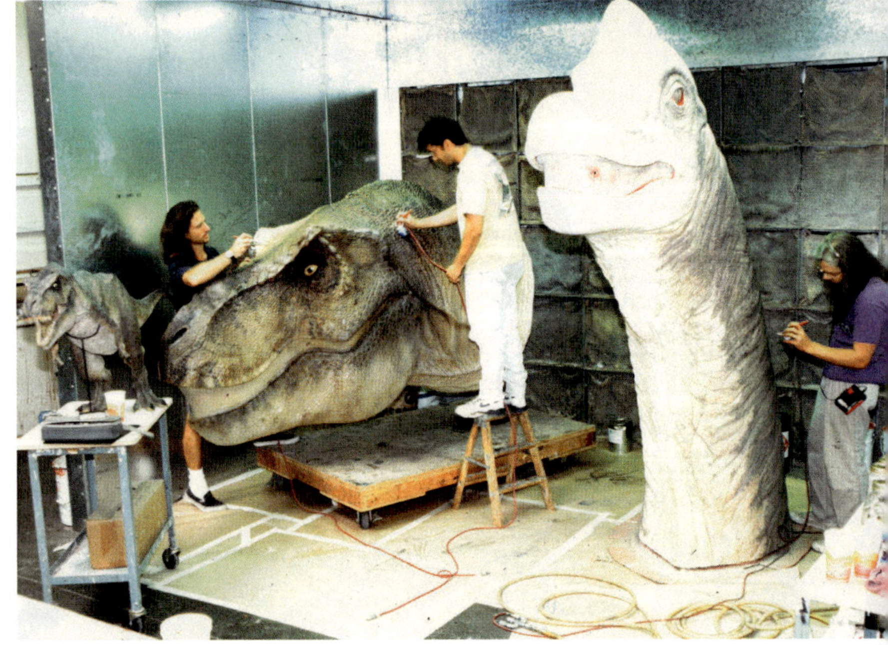

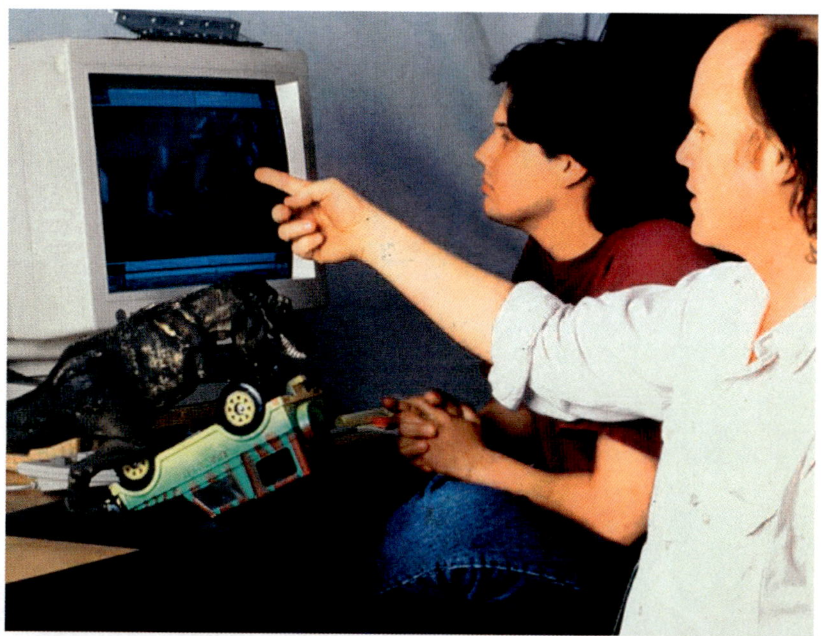

THE OLD AND THE NEW

Stop-motion-animation legend Phil Tippett (near left) rebounded from the personal disappointment that the dinosaurs would be mostly digital by becoming the guru who tied all the F/X disciplines together. He hired a mime to teach the ILM animators how real bodies move and helped create the Dinosaur Input Device. "It was essentially a stop-motion armature that was a very early form of motion capture," Tippett says.

THE RAPTORS

The villainous velociraptors were intelligent and stealthy. For the spine-tingling scene in which they stalk two children in the park's kitchen, Tippett helped the team with an animatic blueprint—a stop-motion video storyboard that captured every shot and angle. From there the artists made use of full-size puppetry, actors in raptor suits (bottom) and postproduction CGI to piece the performances together. "We broke everything down in terms of what Stan's characters could do," Tippett says. "And then we just sort of checkerboarded back and forth between what the capabilities of the different effects were and used them all to their advantage."

DILOPHOSAURUS

To animate the Dilophosaurus that spits venom at Nedry (Wayne Knight), Winston's team created a full-body puppet with three interchangeable heads. The initially unassuming spitter was one of the few dinosaurs to rely completely on Winston's puppeteers for motion and mobility, with no CGI enhancement.

A CHAT WITH NEAL SCANLAN

The Oscar-winning effects maestro of Babe *and* Star Wars *brought his up-close-and-personal creature skill set to the Jurassic universe.* **BY JEFF LABRECQUE**

What do you remember thinking when you saw *Jurassic Park* for the first time?

I have to say, it changed my life. It just redefined visual effects forever and is the same landmark moment as when sound first hit or when color first hit. I had the same gut reaction seeing that film that I had when I was 6 years old and I saw my first Ray Harryhausen movie.

How has the technology evolved in the last 25 years?

We're not really inventing the world in *Fallen Kingdom*, nor are we trying to emulate what Stan and his team had created. In short, what we're trying to do is to make the dinosaurs much more tangible. From all the films, no one has ever been as close and as intimate to the dinosaurs as they are in this film. This is really all about touching them, feeling them breathe, feeling their emotion and being absolutely one-to-one with them.

A good example of something like that is when we see the flashback of Owen meeting the baby Blue, that little Blue puppet that we built. That whole sequence was a joy because Chris Pratt didn't know that this little Blue could bite him, and the puppeteer didn't tell him. So they had this thing where Blue would sort of nestle into his hand and then suddenly take a nip at him, and Chris would just react instantly. It was two actors playing out the scene. It was great.

Was there one particular creature that made you raise your game?

The Indoraptor was to me the really fun one. Because it didn't exist. It's a new DNA strain. In a crazy, egotistic way, you think, "I'm creating a dinosaur." And it's a character that has a certain Nosferatu feel about it, and, you know, I like scaring children. *[Laughs]*

After being transported to San Diego, the T. rex buck escapes and, naturally, tours the city.

THE LOST WORLD 1997

DOUBLE THE FUN

T. Rex *and the* City

DIRECTOR STEVEN SPIELBERG DOUBLED DOWN ON *JURASSIC PARK'S* MOST TERRIFYING DINO AND UNLEASHED A FAMILY OF PREDATORS ON AN UNSUSPECTING SAN DIEGO *By Sean Smith*

H

HERE'S A HOLLYWOOD FACT THAT WAS TRUE in 1997 and has not changed in the past two decades. "Almost all sequels—*Batman Returns*, *Aliens*, *The Godfather Part II*—are darker than the originals," *Jurassic Park* screenwriter David Koepp told *EW* on the eve of the release of the franchise's second installment, *The Lost World: Jurassic Park.* "You can't use the same old tricks—the audience has already seen people being eaten by dinosaurs, so you have to try harder-edged stuff."

Four years earlier *Jurassic Park,* directed by Steven Spielberg and based on Michael Crichton's bestselling novel, had become the highest-grossing film in history, raking in more than $900 million worldwide in its initial release and launching the era of digital effects that we've been living in ever since. (In the intervening years the film has dropped to No. 31, proving that not even a T. rex can withstand a sustained Harry Potter-Marvel-Star Wars-James Cameron attack.)

But back in '97, as Spielberg, Koepp and the *Lost World* cast prepared to swing for the electrified fences one more time, the stakes were higher than a brachiosaurus's neck. Jeff Goldblum, reprising his role as quip-xotic chaos theorist Dr. Ian Malcolm, promised "more danger and more bad stuff for human beings." He wasn't fibbing.

After Isla Nublar was wrecked by human greed, scientific hubris and dinosaurs run amok in the first film, Dr. Malcolm is summoned to the home of Jurassic Park impresario John Hammond (Sir Richard Attenborough) and informed that, hey, guess what? There's a Site B island, Isla Sorna, 80 miles from Isla Nublar, where dinos are living wild, but Hammond's avaricious nephew Peter Ludlow (Arliss Howard) has plans to bring the mega-reptiles to the mainland.

Hammond drafts Malcolm into service to stop Ludlow by informing Malcolm that his girlfriend, paleontologist Dr. Sarah Harding (Julianne Moore), is (surprise!) already on the island. Malcolm sets off to bring her back, unaware that his own daughter Kelly (Vanessa Chester) has stowed away on the trip. Malcolm and team (Richard Schiff, Vince Vaughn) arrive on Isla Sorna just ahead of the bad guys (Howard, Pete Postlethwaite, Peter Stormare), and all paleo hell breaks loose soon afterward.

While *Jurassic Park* explored the dangers of human arrogance, *Lost World* centers mostly on themes of parental instinct, both of the human and reptilian variety. When two T. rex parents attack Malcolm, Harding and Nick Van Owen (Vaughn) in their trailer (in the film's most spectacular white-knuckle set piece), it's not because the creatures are hunting but because the humans have taken a baby T. rex inside to give it medical attention.

Malcolm, meanwhile, has squirreled away his daughter in a treetop blind to try to protect her. Later, when Ludlow succeeds in bringing papa T. rex to San Diego and the beast gets free and begins to wreak havoc, Malcolm and Harding save the day

From left: Julianne Moore, Vince Vaughn, Jeff Goldblum, Vanessa Chester, Pete Postlethwaite, Harvey Jason and Peter Stormare.

Stormare's hunter is attacked by a pack of tiny, vicious Compsognathi.

Dr. Ian Malcolm (Goldblum) meets with John Hammond (Richard Attenborough) at Hammond's New York mansion.

by luring dino dad back to the holding pen of the ship by kidnapping the infant. (There, in a gory slice of poetic justice, Ludlow becomes baby food.)

Both on-camera and off, *Lost World*'s animatronic creatures—a combination of mechanics and digital effects—were not to be messed with. "Oh, the dinosaurs are totally scary," Goldblum said at the time. "Some of the machinery is actually dangerous. You have to turn off your walkie-talkies when you're around them, like on an airplane, because these things might get out of control. And if they get out of control, they can kill. They're very big and very powerful, and they can kill."

It didn't help that Spielberg liked to shoot faster than a gallimimus stampede. "With Spielberg, there are no rehearsals," Goldblum told *EW* at the time. "None....I had an eight-page scene with Richard Attenborough—no rehearsal. Even when you're blocking for the camera, he's like, 'Okay, that's enough; let's shoot.'"

"You want to capture the actors when they taste the words for the first time, when they look at each other for the first time—that's the sort of magic you can only get on a first or second take," Spielberg explained.

Lost World might lack the first-time shock and awe that helped propel *Jurassic Park* into the record books, but it is, as Koepp promised, darker in both content and aesthetics than its predecessor. The body count is higher and bloodier. Spielberg's *Schindler's List* cinematographer, Janusz Kaminski, brings his murky metallic blues and inky blacks to the film's multiple nocturnal scenes. Luckily Spielberg ups the levity too, giving Goldblum some of the franchise's most memorable and trailer-worthy lines, including the instant classic, "Mommy's very angry."

Above all, *Lost World* effectively set up the central thesis that drives the franchise: Some people will always overlook the lessons of the past—to the peril of the rest of us. Thank God it's fun to watch, at least.

▲ The expedition tries to splint a baby T. rex's leg, but things go awry when the angry parents track their offspring to Malcolm, Harding and Nick Van Owen (Vaughn)'s trailer.

> “THE AUDIENCE HAS ALREADY SEEN PEOPLE BEING EATEN BY DINOSAURS, SO YOU HAVE TO TRY HARDER-EDGED STUFF”
>
> *—Screenwriter David Koepp*

▲ The expedition flees a dino attack.

◄ Far left: Harding escapes a velociraptor. Left: After Malcolm and Harding bring the T. rex buck and baby to San Diego, things naturally go wrong. They lure the buck back to the ship by using the baby as bait.

1942-2008

REMEMBERING MICHAEL CRICHTON

In his novel the visionary sci-fi author conjured dinosaurs back to life—but even with Spielberg's help, doing so on film proved a bigger challenge. **BY JEFF LABRECQUE**

WHEN MICHAEL CRICHTON STARTED TO adapt *Jurassic Park* for the big screen, he already had a huge advantage. He had originally conceived his 1990 bestseller, about genetically engineered dinosaurs that attack the guests at an amusement park, as a screenplay (a script that had been unanimously rejected a decade earlier). And more than most writers, the Father of the Techno Thriller understood what movies needed: His first novel, *The Andromeda Strain,* became a successful 1971 film, and Crichton himself went on to direct six motion pictures including the original 1973 *Westworld,* which he also wrote.

But even with Crichton's unique skills and background, the screenplay became an enormous task. Compressing 400 pages of dinosaur chaos, DNA exposition and the underlying theme of science versus nature into a two-hour PG-13 blockbuster tested the author's talents. And patience. "I didn't really want to do the screenplay," Crichton admitted to authors Don Shay and Jody Duncan in *The Making of Jurassic Park.* "I was sick of Malcolm and I was sick of Grant—and I was even sick of the dinosaurs. But I really felt that I knew the dimensions of the story.... So I told Steven [Spielberg], 'I'll do a draft for you and cut it down to budgetable size, but then you're going to want somebody else to polish the characters.'"

Understandably, Crichton's drafts mirrored the novel, which began with a girl being bitten by a dinosaur on a Costa Rican beach and followed the race to prevent stowaway raptors from reaching the mainland by boat. Spielberg opted for a different approach. "Michael had done a wonderful job on the book, both from the scientific perspective and from the adventure side," said the director. "What I wanted to do was boil the book down and choose my seven or eight favorite scenes and base the script around those."

After at least one other (uncredited) writer had a run at the script, the person who finally cracked it was David Koepp (*Death Becomes Her*), who went back to the novel and started from scratch. "I said, 'What are my limitations?' and [Spielberg] said, 'Your imagination,'" Koepp told *The New Yorker* in 1994. "So I really had the freedom to try anything I wanted." He gave the opening a more globe-trotting feel, used "Mr. DNA," an animated character to explain the science, and amplified the wit. Crichton approved: "The script was changed and refined a lot after my draft, in ways that I think are really very good, I should add. It all seems very compatible with my way of thinking—it fits in my mind." Crichton and Spielberg launched the Emmy-winning medical series *E.R.* in 1994, and the author's *Jurassic* follow-up, *The Lost World,* became an instant bestseller and the basis for the 1997 sequel. But he would not live to see this latest iteration of his imagined world. In early 2008 he was diagnosed with lymphoma and died that November at 66. Said Spielberg of his friend's passing: "Michael's talent outscaled even his own dinosaurs."

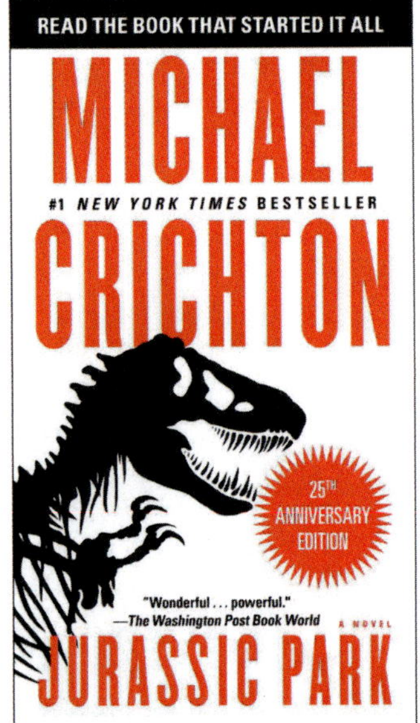

Above: the current mass-market paperback covers for *Jurassic Park,* published in 1990, and *The Lost World,* published in 1995. Both were released before Spielberg's blockbuster films and feature drastically different plots. Right: Crichton and Spielberg on the set of *Jurassic Park* in 1992.

GRANT'S ISLAND VACAY

Welcome (Back) to the Jungle

SAM NEILL'S PALEONTOLOGIST RELUCTANTLY FACED OFF AGAINST YET MORE DINOS—SOME AIRBORNE!—IN THE FIRST JURASSIC FILM WITHOUT STEVEN SPIELBERG DIRECTING *By Sean Smith*

A pack of velociraptors surrounds Dr. Grant (Sam Neill).

L

LET'S START WITH SOME GOOD NEWS: IT'S better than you remember. Released in 2001 at the height of Hollywood's sequel addiction, *Jurassic Park III* was not exactly greeted with open arms. It was the first Jurassic film not based on a Michael Crichton novel and the first not directed by Steven Spielberg. Despite the return of Sam Neill as Dr. Alan Grant—and a pivotal cameo by Laura Dern's paleo-botanist Ellie Sattler—*JPIII* turned in the lowest box office of all the Jurassic films; it made just $368.8 million worldwide—a steep 40 percent plummet from *The Lost World: Jurassic Park* and just a third of the revenue of *Jurassic Park.*

Yet, seen now, divorced from that context, *JPIII* is perhaps the most narratively original, nimble and human-scale entry in the Jurassic canon. Directed by Joe Johnston (*Jumanji*), who had wanted to direct *Lost World* but Spielberg had chosen to—and aided by a script from *Election* scribes Alexander Payne and Jim Taylor—*JPIII* remains the only movie in the franchise that has zero to do with scientific stupidity or sinister corporate forces. Add in the appearance of a ridge-backed killer called a spinosaurus aegyptiacus and the long-awaited close-up reveal of flying pteranodons, and *JPIII* races along with the agile speed of a raptor pack.

The premise this time around is that Dr. Grant and his strapping research assistant Billy Brennan (Alessandro Nivola) have run out of funds for their critical paleo project just as a mysterious couple, Paul and Amanda Kirby (William H. Macy and Téa Leoni), show up and offer them a blank check—provided Grant will fly with them on an adventure tour over Isla Sorna. Grant, promised that the plane will never touch dino-inhabited soil, agrees.

But it turns out that the Kirbys (a) have no money, (b) are divorced and (c) are landing on Isla Sorna to rescue their preteen son Eric (Trevor Morgan), who'd disappeared weeks earlier while parasailing with a family friend over the island. Through a series of events, the plane crashes (of course), and they and the men the Kirbys have hired are stranded.

"When the plane crashes, we were in that fuselage for a week with them rolling us," Macy said in a recent interview with Yahoo! Entertainment. "They rolled it and rolled it. We shot that forever. The actors, we'd sit there between takes and talk to each other: 'I'm gonna go there, then I'm gonna grab that.' We sort of choreographed it so we wouldn't fall on each other as this thing was tumbling along."

How this cast of characters gets stranded on the island is a little too implausible, but what the plot lacks in credibility it makes up for with relatability. Few of us are paleontologists, but we're all either parents or have parents, and the drive to do whatever it takes to save your family, no matter how crazy, anchors *JPIII* in an emotional reality that none of the other *Jurassic* installments can match.

Leoni's performance, it turns out, was informed by real-world events. "In all seriousness, *Jurassic Park* [*III*] was therapeutic

◄ A spinosaurus terrorizes the survivors of a crash landing.

▼ Left: Dr. Grant's what-was-I-thinking face. Right: Amanda Kirby (Téa Leoni), son Eric (Trevor Morgan), Paul Kirby (William H. Macy), Billy Brennan (Alessandro Nivola) and Grant.

for me," she said in a 2012 interview with denofgeek.com. "I'd been through a very traumatic illness with my daughter. And I hadn't actually processed it. I went into mother-bear mode, and I'd been by her, in her bed with her, for 10 days in the hospital...I had kind of buried it. It was so terrifying and so painful, so once she was breathing again and going to survive, I just wanted to move forward. And then Spielberg called with this script....And...when I read it, it was a woman who had lost her child, albeit in a jungle with dinosaurs....I wanted to play it out. I know this sounds totally weird, and I don't think I've ever talked about this, but it was a huge thing for me. Really."

Which is not to say that the film doesn't deliver on all the OMG dinosaur moments that form the bedrock of the franchise. The reveal of the flying pteranodons—in *JPIII's* most spectacular scene, set inside a giant desiccated birdcage—sees a mother ptera plucking young Eric off a bridge and delivering him to her nest of carnivorous babies. As cool as the sequence is, it also raises the question of why these terrifying beasts hadn't appeared in either of the previous films. Turns out, the answer came down to money.

"What happens in movies like this is that when you get into production, you realize you can't afford everything," Johnston told *Movieline* in 2001. "Steven cut the pteranodons out of the first movie, and he figured he'd put them in the second one. Then he had to cut them from the second one."

While the flying reptiles are spotted briefly during the final scene of *Lost World,* they never got the close-up Spielberg wanted, Johnston went on to add. "One of the first things that he said to me in our meetings was that he'd always wanted these flying pteranodons, so he wanted me to come up with something great for them." Mission accomplished, even if no one fully appreciated it—or the rest of the film—at the time.

> "STEVEN [SPIELBERG] CUT THE PTERANODONS OUT OF THE FIRST MOVIE....HE WANTED ME TO COME UP WITH SOMETHING GREAT"
>
> *–Director Joe Johnston*

▲
Left: The Kirbys and Brennan race the spinosaurus as it chases their son and Grant. Right: Grant, Amanda and Eric during another attack.

◀
Although pteranodons were spotted briefly in *The Lost World: Jurassic Park*, the third installment was the first to feature the creatures in a starring role.

▶
The spinosaurus never gets dinner.

EXIT THROUGH THE GIFT SHOP

If dinosaur theme parks existed, they'd surely stock some of these nifty items. Luckily there's no need to venture to a volcanic island to score a cool raptor LEGO set or paleontology kit. **BY SEAN SMITH**

RUBIE'S INFLATABLE COSTUMES
$49.99-$95

Dress up in pure paleo style with these air-puffed outfits from Rubie's Costume Company. Pictured from left: an adult pteranodon costume, an adult Triceratops and a child-size Blue the velociraptor from *Jurassic World.* Owen Grady not included.

FUNKO 'INJURED' IAN MALCOLM ***$25***

Funko figurines are the ultimate expression of fan cool, and nobody (and we mean nobody) is cooler than Jeff Goldblum. This provocatively posed toy recalls everyone's favorite chaos theorist in 1993's original *Jurassic Park,* and it immediately sold out of its limited run at Target. Plastic finds a way...

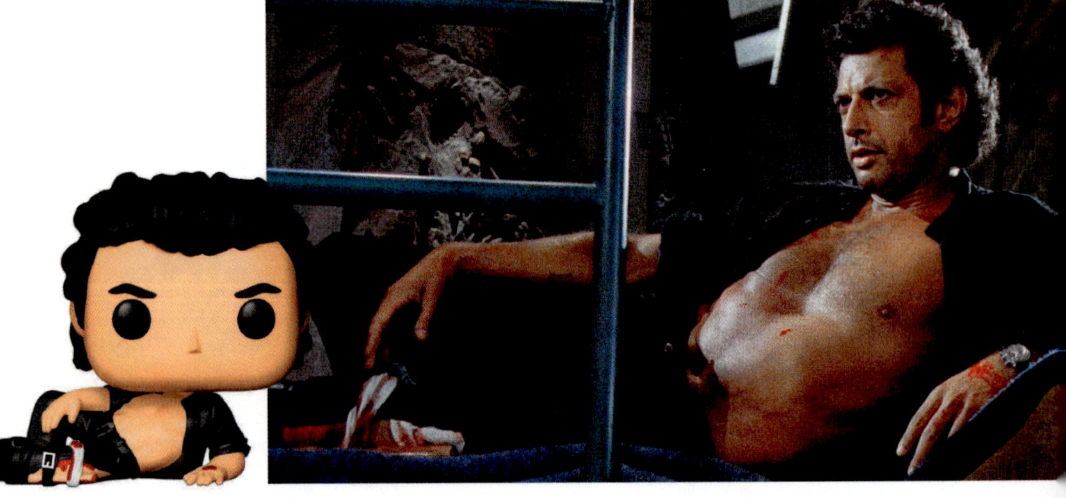

KENNER BUSH DEVIL TRACKER
$25 (used) and up

If the cost of creating your own *Jurassic Park* Jeep is just too steep (pictured, left, a fan's re-creation), there's always this far more affordable option: Kenner's Jurassic Park Vehicle Series 1. Not T. rex-proof.

MATTEL JURASSIC WORLD PLAYLEONTOLOGY KIT ***$24***

Get your science on with this paleontologist excavation set. Includes all the tools needed to dig for dinosaur bones, which can be assembled into a T. rex—which then comes to life. Yes, it's technically for kids, but we won't judge the adult dino enthusiast who might want to pick up a kit or two.

LEGO RAPTOR RESCUE TRUCK ***$19.99***

Want to re-create the sequence in which *Jurassic World: Fallen Kingdom* stars Chris Pratt and Bryce Dallas Howard try to save a velociraptor from an exploding volcano? Now you can—in LEGO. A must-have for the elementary school set.

MATTEL LEGACY COLLECTION ***$26 and up***

Remember those cool dinosaur figures Lowery (Jake Johnson, above, with Lauren Lapkus) kept on his console in the control center in *Jurassic World*? Now you can have them all—plus some he didn't—in this Mattel series of collections. Some are articulated for movement; others are posed dramatically. The perfect toys for a roaring good time.

OPEN TO THE PUBLIC

Risky Business

A WELCOME RELAUNCH BRINGS NEW STARS TO ISLA NUBLAR—ALONG WITH A TOP-FLIGHT DINOSAUR ATTRACTION. WHAT COULD GO WRONG? *By Sean Smith*

JURASSIC WORLD 2015

The two nephews of Claire Dearing (Bryce Dallas Howard) go on an off-the-beaten-path adventure.

B

BIGGER, IT TURNS OUT, IS BETTER. THE 2015 reboot of the Jurassic franchise—22 years after the original *Jurassic Park* stomped on every box office record and 14 years after the underwhelming *Jurassic Park III* seemed to put Hollywood off the island for good—roared back into theaters with the largest (and most lethal) paleo-predator in franchise history, a sparkly new cast, some witty Tracy-Hepburn sexual tension, an enormous $150 million budget and the same thrills and themes that had been putting butts in seats since audiences first gazed up in wonder at a Brachiosaur more than two decades ago.

"There are a lot of people in my generation who dreamed of being filmmakers who would love to have this job, and I feel a responsibility to all of them to make this everything that we all wish it could be," director Colin Trevorrow told *EW* on the New Orleans set of *Jurassic World.* "If I can pull that off, that's my gift back to Spielberg."

It's a fair guess that Spielberg, who served as executive producer on the film, was pretty happy with his present. *Jurassic World* surpassed the success of every other previous installment of the franchise, earning a jaw-dropping $1.67 billion worldwide—for context, that's equal to the box office of *Jurassic Park* and *The Lost World* combined—to become the seventh-highest-grossing film in history.

What's remarkable about that is that the plot of *World* was pretty tried-and-true. Isla Nublar has, at last, become the theme park that John Hammond once dreamed about. Run with impeccable precision by buttoned-up park chief Claire Dearing (Bryce Dallas Howard), Jurassic World teems with tourists, including her two nephews (Nick Robinson and Ty Simpkins), whom she immediately pawns off on her assistant (Katie McGrath) while she attempts to sell a corporate sponsor on shelling out big bucks to present the park's new genetically modified monster. (The Indominus rex, brought to you by Verizon!)

Trouble is, the beast—a top-secret DNA recipe of T. rex, tree frog and cuttlefish (and, spoiler alert: velociraptor)—that towers 40 ft. high and stretches 50 ft. long—may be too clever (and big) for her cage, so Dearing is forced to seek the guidance of behavioral-research expert—and former bad first date—Owen Grady (Chris Pratt). Meanwhile, power-hungry InGen honcho Vic Hoskins (Vincent D'Onofrio) has plans to turn the raptors that Grady has been training into military weapons, and when the Indominus escapes and causes pandemonium on the island, he sees his chance. "It's going to be super-boring," Pratt joked on-set. "It's just, like, us watching dinosaurs for an hour and a half."

Well, it could have been, actually. The plot is *reaaallly* similar to that of just

Owen Grady (Chris Pratt) risks his life for an unlucky raptor tender who falls into the pen.

Dr. Henry Wu (BD Wong, right) meets with his new boss, the CEO and owner of InGen, Simon Masrani (Irrfan Khan).

Claire and Owen discover the wrecked transport that previously contained Claire's two missing nephews.

about every other Jurassic movie. Luckily, what prevents *World* from feeling like a trip down been-there-done-that lane is Pratt himself, who provides the franchise with the hunky smart-aleck heartthrob it never knew it needed and, along with Howard, fizzes up the film with a romantic frisson that had been woefully absent from all the other installments.

Casting Pratt, though, was a huge gamble at the time. *Guardians of the Galaxy* was in production and was far from a guaranteed hit, and Pratt had zero proven bankability as a leading man. "That was a bit of a leap of faith for me," Trevorrow said at the time. "I definitely hadn't seen any of *Guardians.* I found him to be the kind of person I believed to be endearing and funny and warm and yet a total badass who could handle a gun and someone an animal would listen to as a voice of authority." It helped, of course, that Pratt had a certain legendary filmmaker rooting for him. "I felt that he was on the verge of stardom," Spielberg told *EW* at the time. "He is seriously funny and comedically dramatic."

It also helped that audiences, after 14 years of Jurassic-free summers, were hungry to return to Isla Nublar, and, in a case of life imitating film, the Indominus rex was as exciting to ticket buyers as she would have been to Jurassic World tourists. (If, you know, she hadn't killed them outside a Margaritaville first.)

Indeed, the I. rex took center stage in the film's marketing campaign, which kind of bummed Trevorrow out at the time. "I wish we could've kept it a secret," the director said. "But the fact that stuff was leaked through merchandising plays right into what we're doing. Indominus is an abomination and a killer—and on party plates." Such a shame she was dragged off the pier into the water and eaten by that Mosasaurus at the end of the movie. She was just getting started.

Vic Hoskins (Vincent D'Onofrio), the leader of InGen's security team, discusses the military potential of Owen's raptors with the trainer.

The hybrid Indominus rex enters the pteranodon pen, accidentally setting the flying creatures free to terrorize the tourists.

◄ Owen revs up his motorcycle—and his trained velociraptor pack follows.

▼ Claire, Owen, Zach (Nick Robinson) and Gray (Ty Simpkins) watch as Owen's raptor Blue devours Hoskins.

THE PARK IS BACK OPEN

Early concept sketches of key scenes for *Jurassic World* reinvented the faraway island as the idyllic (and functional) theme park. John Hammond would be proud

The Mosasaurus, one of the largest predators of the ancient deep oceans, could open its double-hinged jaws wide enough to devour a great white shark, as in this Jurassic World exhibition.

The toothy standoff between the T. rex and the Indominus rex was set in the rain, a throwback to the T. rex's first appearance in *Jurassic Park*.

Visitors to Isla Nublar can arrive via a slick ship on the dock, a location never pictured in the 1993 film.

Owen Grady (Chris Pratt), Claire Dearing (Bryce Dallas Howard) and Maisie (Isabella Sermon) hide from the Indoraptor.

FALLEN KINGDOM

Dino-Might

CHRIS PRATT AND BRYCE DALLAS HOWARD RETURN TO THE ISLAND OF MISFIT DINOSAURS IN *JURASSIC WORLD: FALLEN KINGDOM*, THE FRANCHISE'S DARKEST, MOST SUSPENSEFUL INSTALLMENT YET. *By Gina McIntyre*

FALLEN KINGDOM 2018

D

DIRECTING THE FIFTH INSTALLMENT IN THE *Jurassic Park* series, J.A. Bayona (*A Monster Calls*, *The Impossible*) might have had reason to worry—no filmmaker wants to retread old dinosaur stomping grounds. So, rather than rehash the past, he blew up the franchise's tried-and-true formula. Literally.

Penned by Derek Connolly and Colin Trevorrow, 2018's *Jurassic World: Fallen Kingdom* sees Isla Nublar destroyed by volcanic activity. The action shifts then to an enormous California estate, where the story's human characters find themselves trapped indoors with a rampaging new terror, the Indoraptor. "The first half, you have a whole dinosaur movie on the island, so you have what you expect from a Jurassic movie," Bayona told *EW*. "Then the second half moves to a totally different environment that feels more suspenseful, darker, claustrophobic and even has this kind of gothic element, which I love."

Bayona established his suspense-movie bona fides with his 2007 feature film debut, the Spanish-language thriller *The Orphanage*, which took place inside a haunted, long-abandoned children's home. The film impressed no less than Steven Spielberg himself with its sublime creepiness. "J.A. knows how to create terror, but he also knows how to orchestrate it so you're not brutalized by it," Spielberg said. "He has the gift of restraint. But when he needs to open up the throttle, he really knows how."

In *Fallen Kingdom*, the filmmaker had plenty of chances to go full throttle. Three years after the events of the last film, the dinosaurs are roaming free on the old grounds of Jurassic World—until the threat of an exploding volcano imperils their continued existence, prompting the Senate to hold hearings on the matter. A suit-and-tied Ian Malcolm (Jeff Goldblum, reprising his fan-favorite role) even turns up to weigh in on the matter.

Explained writer-executive producer Trevorrow, who directed *World*: "You have this extinction-level event on that island, and the world is looking at these creatures that we created and asking, 'Well, what is our right? Do we let them die because we created them and they shouldn't be here in the first place, or do we have a responsibility to save them?'"

Bryce Dallas Howard's executive-turned prehistoric-animal-rights-activist Claire firmly falls in the latter camp. Joining forces with Benjamin Lockwood (James Cromwell), the former partner of Jurassic Park creator John Hammond (Richard Attenborough), Claire launches a rescue mission that will see the animals brought to a U.S. coastal sanctuary. In addition to paleo veterinarian Zia Rodriguez (Daniella Pineda, *The Detour*), Claire recruits raptor trainer extraordinaire Owen Grady (Chris Pratt) to the team by playing on his affections for his favorite creature—and maybe his unresolved feelings for her too. "She appeals to my better self when she brings

▲ The Dinosaur Protection Group lands on Isla Nublar.

◀ The team examines Blue after capturing her. From left: Owen, Franklin Webb (Justice Smith), Claire and Zia Rodriguez (Daniella Pineda).

up Blue because she's still alive," said Pratt. "Claire's going to try to get the dinosaur[s] out of harm's way, and I can join her if I want. And, of course, I do."

When the volcano decimates the island, Owen, Claire and fellow activist Franklin (*The Get Down*'s Justice Smith) are separated from the group and forced to make a daring escape. "We upped the stunt game," Pratt says, alluding to the sequence that sees the trio submerged in the ocean, with Claire and Franklin trapped in a gyrosphere and Owen swimming to their rescue. "It was the result of about a week's worth of work in a water tank," said Pratt. "My eyes got so bloodshot. They were weeping for three straight days because there was so much chlorine."

The heroes make it back to Lockwood's estate, only to discover the dinosaurs are being sold to would-be warlords in an auction organized by Lockwood's financial director Eli Mills (Rafe Spall). "The first film was very clearly about corporate greed," said Trevorrow. "This is just about human greed."

As if that weren't problematic enough, the newly created hybrid dinosaur, the Indoraptor, escapes and runs loose inside the compound, terrorizing Lockwood's little granddaughter Maisie (Isabella Sermon). "That's a kind of hell that we haven't seen in a Jurassic movie," Howard said. "It's surreal to see dinosaurs in that kind of an environment."

Audiences lined up to see *Fallen Kingdom*, with the film taking in upward of $1.3 billion worldwide, even if critics were mixed on the blockbuster. "Pratt flexes his brand of can-do heroism mixed with deadpan sarcasm; and the screenwriters push absurdity to its breaking point, especially in the forehead-slapping final half hour," wrote Chris Nashawaty in his *EW* review. "Until then, though, *Fallen Kingdom* is exactly the kind of monster escapism you want it to be."

For the film's producer Frank Marshall, that escapist appeal is precisely what has made the franchise such a monster hit. "Everybody becomes a kid again when they see dinosaurs," Marshall says. "They're *real*. These existed. And now that we're leaving the island, who knows where we're going to go?"

REPORTING BY TIM STACK

The Indoraptor, a new hybrid dinosaur, stalks through Maisie's bedroom.

Gunnar Eversoll (Toby Jones), begins the auction.

Maisie stands before Lockwood's private collection of dinosaur skeletons.

▶ Heavy-duty trucks cut through a valley that has been reclaimed by nature and dinosaurs. "It was a great chance to explore what the architecture would look like—and not just show beautiful dinosaurs in herds, but to show you what happens if there are carnivores present as well," Nicholson says. "The natural circle of life was great to show."

A WORLD ON FIRE

The striking visual design of the *Jurassic World* sequel evolved from the film's expansive mythology.

BY JEFF LABRECQUE

"Two dinosaurs fighting with a volcano exploding behind them." That was almost the verbatim description of this scene in the film's first treatment. "This was definitely a moment that was never, ever in question of not being in the movie," production designer Andy Nicholson says. The erupting volcano became a crucial influence on every island scene. "When we were shooting, the first question [director J.A. Bayona] would ask is 'Okay, so where's the volcano now?' We thought the audience would always be able to recalibrate themselves from where the volcano is."

This isn't the Museum of Natural History but the private collection of Benjamin Lockwood (James Cromwell), John Hammond's former InGen partner who has his own fascination with dinosaurs. Not only are there assembled skeletons, but Lockwood has stuffed dinosaurs as well. "J.A. chose a whole series of dinosaurs that you haven't seen in the movie before—in any of the franchises before—and put them into dioramas and gave them each a little story," Nicholson says.

BEHIND THE SCREAMS

Director J.A. Bayona and his talented filmmaking team, including creature effects creative supervisor Neal Scanlan, utilized a combination of practical and special effects to bring the dinosaurs of *Jurassic World: Fallen Kingdom* to life. **BY SEAN SMITH AND TIM STACK**

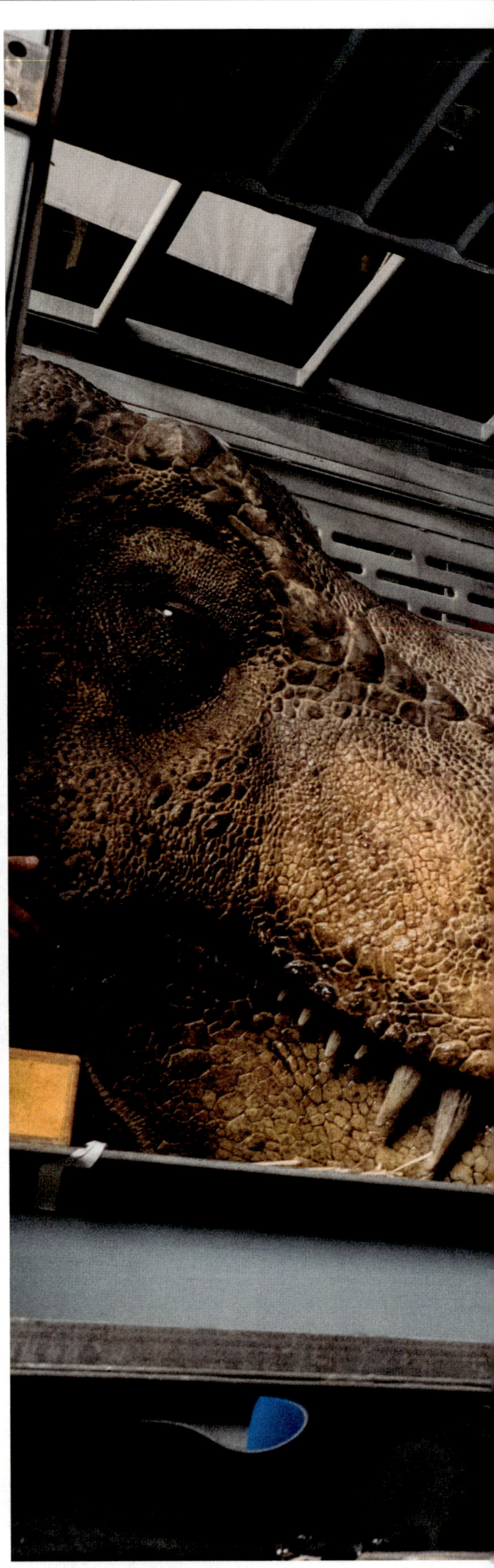

▲
J.A. Bayona stands with Isabella Sermon, who plays Maisie, in the private dinosaur collection of James Cromwell's Benjamin Lockwood. Twenty-five years earlier, a young Bayona had watched Steven Spielberg's *Jurassic Park* and had been set on a path that led him to *Fallen Kingdom*. "When I saw that Brachiosaurus come alive," he wrote, "I knew that I was witnessing a moment that would stand the test of time. For me it was proof that from then on, whatever idea I imagined, no matter how crazy it might seem, it would be possible to capture it onscreen in a realistic way."

▶
The T. rex: tagged and caged. Neal Scanlan (seated) cues up a scene for Chris Pratt's Owen Grady.

▶ Bryce Dallas Howard's Claire Dearing and Justice Smith's Franklin Webb look frightened in the rig that stood in for the gyrosphere.

▼ The Indoraptor's arm wielded by animatronic technician Duncan MacLeod. "It's great when you can work with animatronics and with puppets rather than tennis balls," says Pratt.

Pratt says Bayona brought his signature style to *Fallen Kingdom,* including "a sense of pacing and suspense."

WHERE FACTS MEET SCIENCE FICTION

Real-life paleontologist Jack Horner helps to make the Jurassic Park films as authentic as possible **BY JEFF LABRECQUE**

WHEN STEVEN SPIELBERG WANTED A dinosaur expert to consult on *Jurassic Park,* he didn't have to dig too deep. Jack Horner was Michael Crichton's inspiration for Dr. Grant, and the author name-dropped the noted paleontologist in his 1990 bestseller. And so after a phone call from Spielberg—Hollywood's own John Hammond—Horner left his research to bring dinosaurs back to life.

"He wanted me to work with the artists and make sure that the *Jurassic Park* dinosaurs were as accurate as they could be," says Horner, whose 1988 book *Digging Dinosaurs* produced groundbreaking evidence about dinosaur behavior and biology. "They wanted me to make sure that everything was in paleontological order." The *Jurassic* team made changes, including eliminating forked tongues from the raptors, when Horner asked. "Steven was good about that," Horner says. "If we had scientific evidence for something being one way or another, he would change it." Most of the time.

Horner had hoped that the raptors would be feathered and much more colorful, but a feathered dinosaur was beyond the capabilities of stop-motion and the nascent CGI technology of the time. "He basically said that Technicolor dinosaurs weren't as scary as his brown and gray ones were," he adds.

Similarly, the T. rex was bigger and faster than Horner recommended, and he came to set with a perfect smile (though in *Jurassic Park III* the dinosaurs' mouths reflected signs of wear and tear).

The franchise's embrace of lab-made hybrid species had led to "new" dinosaurs that are much closer to the creatures that once walked the earth. "I tell people that Indominus rex [from *Jurassic World*] is the most accurate dinosaur ever made," Horner says.

Horner is currently leading an effort to retro-engineer a bird back to a dinosaur. He says, "If we're lucky, we'll have a dinosaur in the next couple of years." Buy your park tickets now.

▲ Left: Dr. Sattler (Laura Dern), Dr. Malcolm (Jeff Goldblum) and Dr. Grant (Sam Neill) watch a dinosaur hatch in *Jurassic Park*. Right: The new lab as seen in *Jurassic World: Fallen Kingdom*.

◀ A mosquito bearing dinosaur DNA captured in amber was a *Jurassic Park* prop.

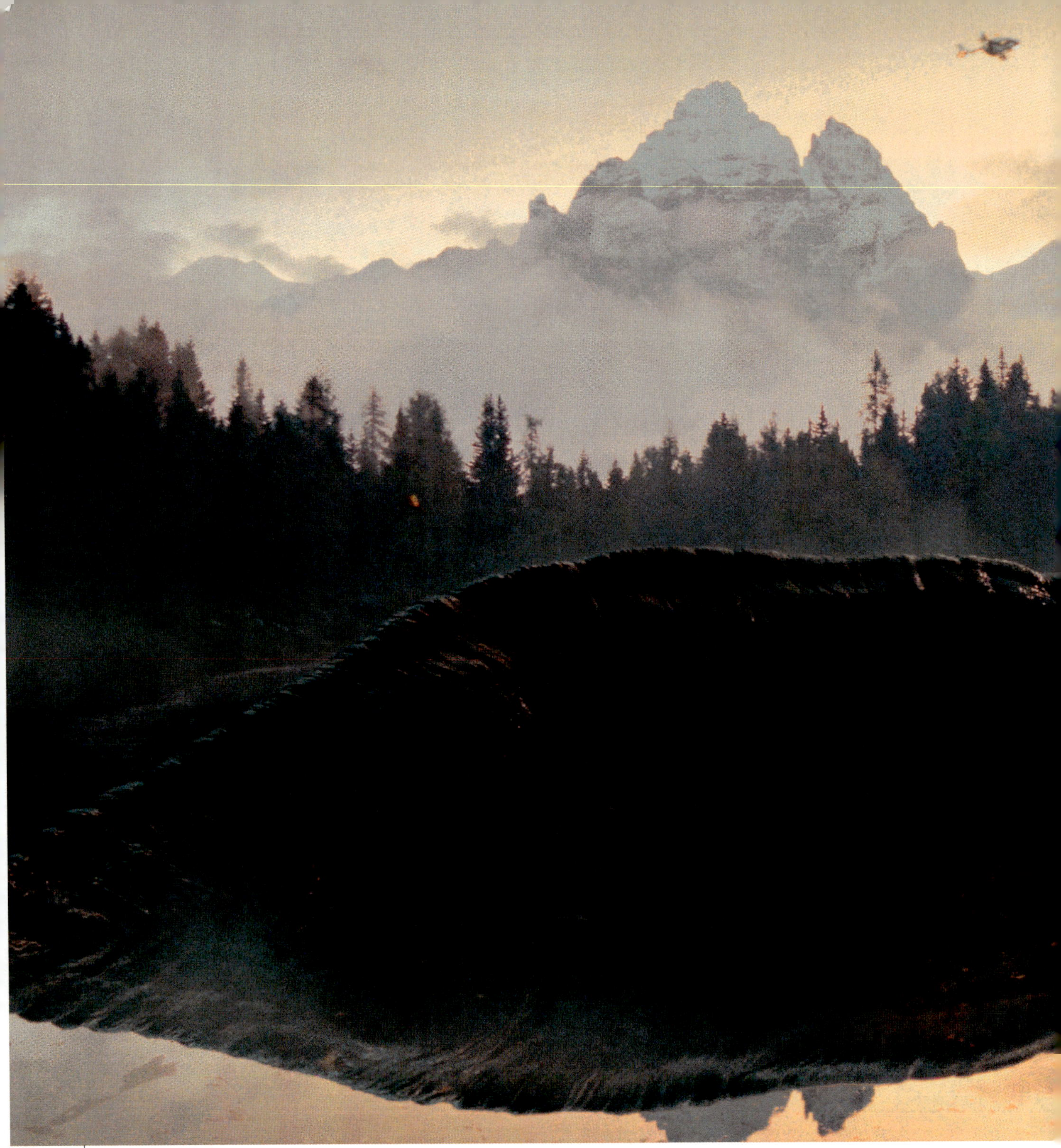

JURASSIC PARK
Editorial Director Kostya Kennedy
Edition Editor Alyssa Smith
Editor, People + EW Books Allison Adato
Editor Gina McIntyre (2018 edition)
Art Director Ronnie Brandwein-Keats, Chuck Kerr
Photo Editor Robert Conway (2018 edition), Rachel Hatch (2022 edition)
Writers Bill Keith, Jeff Labrecque, Gina McIntyre, Sean Smith, Tim Stack, Keith Staskiewicz
Reporters Andréa Ford, Daniel S. Levy
Copy Desk Joanann Scali (Chief), James Bradley (Deputy), Ellen Adamson, Gabrielle Danchick, Richard Donnelly, Shakthi Jothianandan, Matt Weingarden (Copy Editors)
Production Designer Peter Niceberg (2018 edition)
Premedia Executive Director Richard Prue
Senior Manager Romeo Cifelli
Manager Rob Roszkowski
Premedia Trafficking Supervisor Chris Sprague
Premedia Imaging Specialist Randy J. Manning
Color Quality Analyst Pamela Powers
Imaging Production Associates Franklin Abreu, Ana Kaljaj
Research Director Céline Wojtala

DOTDASH MEREDITH PREMIUM PUBLISHING
Vice President & General Manager Jeremy Biloon
Vice President, Group Editorial Director Stephen Orr
Director, Brand Marketing Jean Kennedy
Associate Director, Brand Marketing Bryan Christian
Senior Brand Manager Katherine Barnet

Editorial Director Kostya Kennedy
Creative Director Gary Stewart
Director of Photography Christina Lieberman
Editorial Operations Director Jamie Roth Major
Manager, Editorial Operations Gina Scauzillo

SPECIAL THANKS
Brad Beatson, Samantha Lebofsky, Kate Roncinske

DIGITAL
President Leah Wyar
Editor in Chief, Entertainment Weekly Mary Margaret

A Dreadnoughtus has room to stretch out in *Jurassic World Dominion*.

PHOTO CREDITS

COVER: Pratt, Howard: Frank Ockenfels/Universal/ Legendary; (c) 2018 Universal Pictures and Amblin Entertainment, Inc. and Legendary Pictures Productions, LLC. All Rights Reserved(2); Goldblum, Dern, Neill: Universal (3); T-Rex: Universal Pictures and Amblin Entertainment; **BACK COVER:** (from top): Universal Pictures and Amblin Entertainment; Universal; **Pg 1:** Universal Pictures and Amblin Entertainment, Inc. and Legendary Pictures Productions, LLC.; **Pg 2-3:** Universal Pictures and Amblin Entertainment; **Pg 4-5:** (clockwise from top): Universal; Aram Papazyan/Stocktrek Images/Getty Images; Bernard Weil/Toronto Star via Getty Images; **Pg 6-7:** Universal Pictures and Amblin Entertainment; **Pg 8-9:** John Wilson/Universal Pictures and Amblin Entertainment (2); **Pg 10-11** (clockwise from top): Universal Pictures and Amblin Entertainment; John Wilson/Universal Pictures and Amblin Entertainment; Universal Pictures and Amblin Entertainment; **Pg 12-13:** John Wilson/Universal Pictures and Amblin Entertainment (4); **Pg 14-15:** Matthias Clamer; **Pg 17:** Vera Anderson/WireImage/Getty; **Pg 19:** Steve Schofield/Contour/Getty; **Pg 20:** John Wilson/Universal Pictures and Amblin Entertainment **Pg 21** (from top): Universal Studios and Amblin Entertainment; Jaimie Trueblood/Universal; John Wilson/Universal Pictures and Amblin Entertainment (2); Jaimie Trueblood/Universal **Pg 22-23** (clockwise from left): Universal Pictures and Amblin Entertainment (2); John Wilson/ Universal Pictures and Amblin Entertainment; **Pg 24:** Denise Truscello/Contour/Getty; **Pg 25** (from left): Christopher Patey/Contour/Getty; Corey Nickols/Contour/Getty; **Pg 26-27:** Universal; **Pg 28-29** (clockwise from top left): Universal; Industrial Light & Magic/Universal; Universal; **Pg 30-31:** Universal; **Pg 32-33:** Universal (3); **Pg 34-35:** 4 Universal Pictures and Amblin Entertainment; 3 Universal; dinosaur silos: Universal(6); Dimorphodon, Ankylosaurus: Amblin Entertainment (2); **Pg 36-37:** 1, 2 Universal; dinosaur silos: Universal(7); Mosasaurus: Amblin Entertainment; **Pg 38-39:** Universal; **Pg 40-41:** Universal(3); **Pg 42-43:** Goldblum, Dern, Peck: Murray Close/ Universal; Universal(2); **Pg 44-45:** Universal(3); **Pg 46-47:** Universal(3); **Pg 48-49**: Universal(4); map: Amblin Entertainment; **Pg 50-51**: Universal; **Pg 52-53:** Universal(4); **Pg 54-55:** Universal(4); Scanlan: Giles Keyte/Universal; **Pg 56-57:** Universal; **Pg 58-59:** Universal(3); **Pg 60-61:** Universal(4); **Pg 63:** Universal; **Pg 64-65:** Universal; **Pg 66-67:** Universal(3); **Pg 68-69:** Universal(4); **Pg 70:** dinosaur costumes: Seth Mayer/Rubie's (3); Goldblum: Universal; Funkofigure: Funko; **Pg 71:** Playleontology, mini dinosaurs: Mattel(2); Raptor Rescue: LEGO; Bush Devil Tracker Jeep: Baptiste Coudert; custom Jeep: Rubens Alarcon/Alamy; Jurassic World: Chuck Zlotnick/ Universal; **Pg 72-73:** Universal; **Pg 74-75:** Pratt: Universal; Chuck Zlotnick/Universal(2); **Pg 76-77:** Pratt, Sy, Chuck Zlotnick/Universal; Universal(3); **Pg 78-79:** Amblin Entertainment(3); **Pg 80-81:** Universal; **Pg 82-83:** Universal(2); **Pg 84-85:** Universal(3); **Pg 86-87:** Universal(3); **Pg 88-89** (from left): Giles Keyte/Universal; Universal; **Pg 90-91** (from top): Jaimie Trueblood/Universal; Giles Keyte/ Universal (2); **Pg 92-93:** Universal(3); **Pg 94-95:** Universal **Pg 96:** Universal

“THESE CREATURES WERE HERE BEFORE US. AND IF WE'RE NOT CAREFUL, THEY'RE GONNA BE HERE AFTER”

—Dr. Ian Malcolm

Made in the USA
Las Vegas, NV
04 June 2022